M000093424

Just Don't Call Me

Margaret

A Journey from Depression to Divinity

By

Margie Sherman

Copyright © 2019 Margie Sherman

Publisher's Cataloging-in-Publication Data
Sherman, Margie.

Journey from depression to divinity. You make a difference in the world, what you do matters. You matter. / Margie Sherman.

1st edition
p.   cm.
ISBN: 978-0-9982199-2-9
1. biography 2. spirituality 3. healing 4. self-help 5. depression
920 dc23
G320 D811.xA3-S 2019
LCCN 2019936896

All rights reserved. No part of this publication may be reproduced, stored in a retrieval system, or transmitted in any form by any means, electronic, mechanical, recording or otherwise, without the prior written permission of the author.

Cover Design by Marcella Fox
www.MarcellaFox.com

Fernhead Publishing ™
Suwanee, GA 30024

fernheadpub@gmail.com
http://www.fernheadpublishing.com

Printed in the United States of America

Book Reviews

When I began reading Margie's book, I was transported into her living room, sitting across from her like a trusted friend, as she courageously told me her life story. I highly recommend this book to everyone, especially those who are depressed and feeling alone.

Larraine Brannon
Certified Emotion Code Practitioner

Margie's deeply personal story chronicles her journey from grief to fulfillment and from trauma to forgiveness. She kept forging ahead while each day found her wondering how she could keep going. I was moved by her touching account of finding love and letting the light within in her shine brightly. Her message is a testament to her faith and empowerment.

Cheryl Hunter
Trauma Survivor and Life Coach

A brutally honest look at a lifetime of sexual, physical and psychological abuse, it's also about love, forgiveness and a belief in a universal power that has a plan for everyone. This book could be written by countless thousands of people that feel they have no voice. Thank you Margie for giving us that voice.

Roger Phifer
Reiki Master

Margie Sherman has beautifully and powerfully illuminated her healing journey from the depths of depression to the heights of divine Grace. It is clear that while her early life experiences and relationships dampened her inner light, it was never extinguished. I was deeply touched by her courage, her honesty and her dedication to reclaiming the truth of her being. Her story reflects her indomitable Spirit, a willingness to do the challenging work of forgiveness and her surrender to that mysterious force that calls us to awaken to the magnificence of our true Self.

Karen Axnick
Spiritual Counselor

A beautiful beacon of hope. Poignant illustrations of a hero's journey through deep depression and overwhelm, and divinity's hand of Love that always holds and guides no matter appearances through great hardships and challenges.

Theresa Gooch
Love Transformed Coach

Transforming raw innocence to pure eloquence, Margie's own compelling reality and her strength serve to inspire and motivate those who find themselves in darkness. She exemplifies that with courage, determination and sheer will, one can find the blessed light and survive. I truly believe this autobiography will affect and change lives, which is a mission that Margie wholeheartedly embraces. Her honest tears become drops of healing and holy water that flows over the reader, page by page.

Peggy Barnes
Published Poet

Margie is an incredibly wise, kind and beautiful angel on this planet. She has a spirit that creates an easy space for the deepest type of release work and forgiveness. She truly lives a life of compassion and generosity and her story of abuse, love, loss and redemption is a vividly portrayed lesson in surrender. Don't be surprised if you find yourself transformed by the time you finish her book.

Crystal Henderson
Crystal Henderson Agency

One of the most crucial life skills to be able to make the most of a life is resilience which comes through a blend of wisdom, tenacity, an ability to endure what cannot be changed, and a relentlessness of Spirit that just doesn't allow you to give up, no matter how hard life is. Margie's story, so vulnerably and beautifully shared in Just Don't Call Me Margaret, is a real life manual on how to employ massive resilience, in tandem with more than a little Grace, to deal with a life full of steady challenges, love, loss and hard won forgiveness. It's an inspiring read to match an inspiring life!

Geoff Laughton
International best-selling author of
Built to Last Designing & Maintaining a Passionate Loving and Lasting Relationship and *Building a Conflict Proof Relationship*

Just Don't Call Me Margaret impresses my soul with its poignancy and simplicity. Margie's no-fluff story telling brings home the fact that abuse is ubiquitous, often occurring at home, a place that should be a safe haven.

This powerful story of healing needs to be heard and will touch the lives of many. It is a beautiful reminder that hope and love are around the corner, and everything we do matters.

Lisa Andrews
Auric Energy Healer and
Ordained Minister

Margie struck me as formidable from the moment I met her. Reading *Just Don't Call Me Margaret* does more than enhance my first impression of a stunning woman. The book led me down the path of a woman's life that I could not have imagined. The life-long pain and sorrow that Margie was able to endure and overcome with Divinity is moving and inspiring. And the ability to forgive and thrive is pure magic.

Dawn Cushman
Appellate Attorney

Dedicated to:

My Beloved Grandmother

TABLE OF CONTENTS

Prologue

I am so grateful I didn't commit suicide. As you
accompany me in the journey of these pages my
intention is that you understand that although
difficulties befall each of us in life, there are also kernels
of light and love that shine through. If I had taken the
path of killing myself through whatever means I often
thought of, all the goodness of life would have passed me
by. You have more strength than you know. You too can
survive a lot of hurt. Just keep putting one foot in front
of the other. Each new day brings new opportunities to
find the love and happiness that you desire and truly
deserve.

When I first wrote the seeds of this book, it was
part of an interactive paper I wrote as my final project
for my degree – a Master's thesis of sorts, in abbreviated
form. Throughout the ensuing years I have tried several
times to put the finishing touches on the book. However,
I would find myself getting severely depressed as I wrote
about my depression and thoughts of suicide. I would
just have to put my writing aside and so assumed my
book would never be written.

Now 18 years later I find myself in a different
emotional space. The depression is still hard to write
about, but this time I find I must tell the story. It calls

me. When emotions get the best of me I turn to food. I know that is part of stuffing my feelings, but I haven't reentered the same abyss as the dark pit of my depression. I have procrastinated so many times that a little overeating seems surmountable, at least in the short term.

Much of this book is about my relationship with my mother. Whenever I would get depressed, she used to say, "Chin up." I have learned to hate that phrase but in a sense it put her view on life in perspective. She didn't allow grief or pain to deter her. There may be some usefulness in it I suppose. Now I just joke about it with family. "Hang in there" is another oft used phrase. Most of these sayings don't do much to make a person feel better.

This book is written to inspire and help each of you know that you are a wonderful, unique human being. Your voice matters, just as mine does. Current societal movements have shown that we cannot be silenced any longer. And I have found that if you continue to wade through the muck of your emotions, even if it takes a long time, there is much more to experience on the other side.

So keep moving forward. Seek help where you can. Keep marching. "Chin up." "Hang in there." You are resilient and tougher than you think. You can and need to survive. The world needs you.

Many blessings,

Margie Sherman, February 2019
Eugene, Oregon

PART I

1969

I sit staring out the window, seeing nothing, trapped in my thoughts and trying to decide what to write. I am remembering this story, wanting to record it just as it happened, yet struggling with the pain of it all.

It was during one of my many hospitalizations. I was sharing a room with someone else. Back in the 1960s and '70s private rooms were hard to come by. My roommate was a small woman with mousy brown hair. She appeared quite young but the haunted, vacant look on her face was what struck me. She barely spoke. I happened to mention to the nurse that I was curious why this woman seemed so forlorn.

"Oh, yes" said the nurse. "She is only 13."

The problem? We were in the maternity ward.

There were no patient privacy rules back then, so the nurse went on to tell me "Her father is the baby's father. Her parents plan to raise the child as her sister. They want to punish her for getting pregnant."

I knew I had been sedated but upon awakening I struggled with this news. I lived in a civilized society. I knew it happened in other countries, but did not expect to be confronted with that here. Who would be so cruel as to make their 13 year old give birth to a child under such circumstances? It deeply saddened me and shaped my viewpoint for years to come.

This experience had a profound effect on me. It brought back old memories of my own. Although I didn't realize it at the time, this encounter put a chink in the wall that I had built to protect my heart. I had a difficult childhood and as an adult had begun having frequent nightmares and flashbacks. Sometimes I would wake up crying, angry and inconsolable. Depression stuck to me like glue.

Depression

Paralysis. Despair. Hopelessness. Powerlessness. Disconnection. Low self- esteem. These are common words used to describe depression. A few dictionaries' definitions include sadness, gloom and dejection. My experience of it included not only each of these things but an all pervasive feeling of being unloved, of being unlovable. Many events led to my depression; many others kept me stuck there.

There is a great deal of literature written about depression. It has become a subject of vast research, the topic of numerous books and articles and a reason for long-term therapy. In 1953 Greenspan writes "Depression is a condition endemic to women as a group. Depression is the feminine symptom to end all symptoms."[i] It took many years and hours of therapy before I began to comprehend the ramifications of how depression had affected my life, my health and the lives of my children.

The earliest memories I have of feeling like my world was collapsing and I was going down a black hole with no expectation of coming out was the year my grandmother died. I was 13. My grandmother was the one person I trusted. The one who truly mothered me. My greatest spiritual teacher. She was warm and caring, always giving me hugs and telling me I was special. She had also told me that I had a guardian angel who would be with me always.

I was devastated when she died. I could not speak of her for almost ten years without bursting into tears. Along with losing her significant influence in my life, there were other losses too. My brother whom I idolized got married that same year. Several months later my family made a cross country move from the cold north of Minnesota to warm Texas. I lost everything that I knew to be safe. I have always claimed it was the worst year of my life.

Call Me Mother

At an early age mother told my brother and me that we were not to call her mommy or mom, but instead Mother. It represented respect. She told us that we were to respect and love her because she was our mother. It created a sort of distance between us. She never was one to be warm and cuddly.

I remember as a baby standing in my crib and crying, screaming actually. No one ever came. I heard later that Mother believed children should not be comforted after being put to bed. "They will just cry until they get tired enough to fall asleep," she used to say. She wasn't in the habit of ever hugging us or being nurturing. All the baby pictures I ever saw of me showed a young child looking afraid and tearful.

My mother was a tall, attractive woman, slender and straight backed. Correct posture was very important to her. As we got older she used to hit us in the back to make us stand up straighter. She expected her children to reflect a positive image of her, so we were always scrubbed and our clothes were clean although many of mine were hand-me-downs. She later told me I didn't have a store bought dress until I was five years old. She spoke very proudly of this fact whenever she talked about it.

She had been one of six children born to a dirt farmer in west Texas. She was the third child with two older brothers whom she idolized. Her father sent her off at age 16 with 50 cents in her pocket. She lived with one of her teachers as she finished high school. There she learned how to sew. She was a meticulous seamstress which was helpful in keeping those hand-me-downs in shape.

Mother had a very conflicted relationship with her primary family and I only met them a few times. She had moved away when she married my dad and rarely went to see them. When I was about six or seven she took my brother and me on the train from Minnesota to Texas to visit them. I suffered from severe motion sickness which made the long trip unbearable. When we arrived, there were lots of cousins to play with since her other siblings had all stayed close to home. I barely remember her parents.

****

I had been an exuberant child with bundles of energy. My mother believed that children should be seen and not heard, so conflict between us began very early in my life. She never cried or expressed any emotion in front of us that I recall other than anger. She frequently spanked us with a belt, one that belonged to my grandfather I think. I remember one time when she was spanking my brother and I began crying. I was probably about six or seven years old. She became enraged and turned the belt toward me. "I'll give you something to cry about" she said flinging the belt at my legs. Thwack, thwack, thwack. It stung for a long time and caused welts on my legs and butt.

My exuberance began to dissipate.

The belt was brought out quite often. One time she took me to the shoe store and the salesman asked if I was being abused. My legs were covered with bruises. She told him I was just a clumsy child and fell down a lot. I wanted to tell him what really happened at home but was too afraid to say anything. One look from Mother told me to keep my mouth shut.

She expected our house to be clean at all times. If just the daily newspaper was on the floor, she would think the house unsuitable for company. Because she was the only one in her circle of friends to have children, people frequently congregated at our house. That made it easier for mother so she did not have to get a babysitter whenever she went out. My brother and I did the dishes each night after supper. If we didn't get them sparkling clean she would make us wash and dry them all over again.

Mother would clean the house on the weekends in her bra and underpants. I remember that always making me uncomfortable. She didn't want to get any of her clothes dirty. She showed me that in order to get the floors clean you had to be down on your hands and knees and get to every crevice. The floors were to be washed in the corners with a toothbrush. With the carpet I was shown to go along the baseboards with the vacuum attachment. Dirt was clearly the enemy!

When I was a young girl Mother had several friends. She laughed with them a lot. I remember sitting on the floor under the kitchen table as she and other women had coffee on Saturday mornings. I loved to listen to them talk and sometimes whisper. I usually got in trouble for eavesdropping.

Minnesota

When I was five we went to live with my father's parents in Minnesota. We had been living across the country and took a long car ride to get there. I barely remember stopping at Yellowstone on the way. Grandma and Grandpa lived in the southern part of the state in a small, rural community. There was not even a post office. They felt guilty that their second son had not proven to be a worthy husband. They had taken pity on their daughter-in-law and asked her to bring us and come live with them.

That's when my grandmother became my lifeline. She welcomed us with open arms. She taught me word games and we would play them while cooking or doing the dishes. She would say, "If your grandmother went to China, what would she take in her suitcase?" I would have to respond with words that corresponded to every letter in the alphabet. It was fun to come up with outlandish things that she would have in her suitcase. I remember laughing with her as we did this. She also imparted spiritual lessons from many different perspectives. Having captured my imagination, I spent many hours talking to her and listening for her pearls of wisdom. I never tired of sitting near her and hearing her stories about anything and everything.

Our grandparents were some of the original settlers in the community and they were very involved in church. Grandpa was the choir director as well as an elder and grandma was the organist and pianist. We were expected to always look perfect and act perfectly because Mother wanted us to look good to others. What others thought of us, or more importantly *her*, was very important. She must have felt awkward as a single adult at a time when divorce was not common or acceptable. This was the 1950s and single adulthood was not in vogue. Women were thought of in a negative light if they didn't stay married. And already married women were worried that their husbands might stray if an attractive, single woman was nearby.

****

The old rope swing which hung from the huge oak tree in the front yard of the farmhouse became my go-to place. The tree was very tall with thick, craggy bark and the lowest branches were too tall to climb up to. The swing was just a worn piece of two by four held up with a very thick rope. It had been there for many years and my aunt and uncle had played on it along with my dad. It hung over the lawn and if I turned just the right way, I could pump my legs really hard and pretend that I would soar over the driveway below.

I would sing at the top of my lungs and played outside much of the time. Mother always said that I had too much energy and exuberance for my grandma to handle so I needed to be good and stay out of her way. Grandma taught me all the verses to "Que Sera Sera" and it became my favorite song. I sang it over and over and never tired of its promise for the future. I also knew all the church songs and I enjoyed singing those too. These moments were very precious to me.

One of my favorite things as a young girl was when the Bookmobile would come. The driver, an older gentleman, would pull into my grandparents' driveway and park for a long time while grandma and I looked at all the books available. The bus was lined with bookshelves just like a small library with children's books, adult fiction, nonfiction, etc. It was grandma's connection to the outside world since the farmhouse was many miles from any town. She so looked forward to seeing that big bus pull into the yard every two weeks. She and the driver had obviously known each other for many years and had lots to talk about. It was during this time that I developed a life-long love of books. During the summer I read as many as I was allowed to check out at a time.

Grandma was a gentle soul, a student of Native American life and an avid bird watcher. She spoke several languages, knew about palm reading, and deeply loved the Divine. To keep me busy in the summer she got me to dig dandelions in the huge front yard so we could eat the greens for dinner. She pointed out birds in the trees, but I had a difficult time seeing them. I had worn glasses since I was 18 months old but even with them my vision was less than perfect. She urged me to be careful when I climbed the apple trees, but didn't tell me not to. She taught me about all the shapes in the clouds and pointed out many different constellations in the night sky. We would lay down in the grass in the large front yard and stare up at the stars. She instilled in me a wonder and awe of all of nature and a curiosity about everything.

Grandma gave me guidance and assurance that God was up there in the heavens looking down on us all. Her reverence was profound and I felt comforted by what she told me. She taught me to say my prayers each night before bed and bless all those around us who needed help. I believe it was her care for other people that planted the earliest seeds in my life of fighting for the underdog.

The women's circle from church would meet at grandma's house each month for lunch. It was a fancy affair with antique porcelain name plates which I was allowed to print out. Grandma took each opportunity to teach me how to set the table correctly with all the necessary forks and spoons. Over half a century later I still remember each of those older women by name, many of whom were distant relatives of my grandparents. Everyone enjoyed the gathering and I had fun watching them.

My grandfather worked each day in the nearest big city and managed his small dairy farm in his spare time. He was very clearly the leader of the family and we all did what he said. He expected dinner to be served each evening at 5:30 pm and if it wasn't ready on time, he would get very angry. He made sure we children behaved.

Work and chores were expected of us each day and doing well in school was highly prized. I remember grandpa giving me a dime for every "A" I got on my report card until he complained that was the only grade I ever got. I fondly remember the years we lived on the farm. I have few memories of my mother during this period however.

One memory I do have is about a gentleman who worked for grandpa in town but would come over to the house frequently. He liked to have me sit on his lap while we watched television. While I don't have clear memories of abuse since I was only about 5 or 6, I remember hiding in grandpa's closet in the dark, frightened of this man. This happened more than once. One day he was sitting on the couch with mother and I walked along and kicked him in the shins. He kicked me back with his big heavy shoes. Obviously I didn't like him very much.

Our grandparents gave us a good foundation of work and play. They set strict examples of good living and devotion to God. After a few years in the farmhouse we moved across the highway to our own home. Mother expressed her pleasure at being out from under my grandma's prying eyes. She liked to entertain her friends, go out occasionally and now had more freedom to do so. Several nearby neighbors would come for coffee on Saturday mornings. My brother and I were told she was going out for ice cream when she would leave us alone to be with friends in the evening. They really went out drinking. There was no crime in the area to speak of and no one seemed worried about us. It was a time of innocence, or so we thought.

Dad's Visit

My father left our family when I was eighteen months old. Alone with two children mother was forced to work outside the home and was continually waiting for my father's return. He did return, usually about one week each year, drunkenly reassuring us all how much he loved us, taking whatever money might be available and leaving again.

One summer day during one of those visits when I was eight, dad had been sleeping late. He had been up until the wee hours the night before. I had heard my parents arguing which they frequently did when he was drinking. The sounds had awakened me. I was playing quietly in my room so as not to disturb him. Mother was at work.

Dad got out of bed completely naked to go to the bathroom and I saw his erect penis. I remember how its size scared me. He called to me and asked me to come into the bedroom and lie down with him. His body reeked of stale alcohol and cigarettes. He offered to rub my back, something I especially loved. As he lifted my shirt he told me over and over how beautiful I was and how proud he was of me. My skin was sprinkled with small moles and freckles which he gently teased me about.

As I lay on my stomach he began moving his body back and forth along my leg. My stomach churned as feelings that something was not right enveloped me. I was afraid to move. Then dad pulled down my panties and lay down on my back.

I asked timidly, "What are you doing? Why are you doing that?"

After a few moments he penetrated me. The pain was unlike anything I had ever known. I felt confused, scared and completely shattered.

As I cried out, he said "Shush. It's okay. I just want to show you how much I love you. You love me too, don't you? Everything will be just fine."

I still remember staring out the window beside the bed at the trees, their leaves blowing in the wind. I wasn't sure what was happening. After several minutes he grunted and pulled away. I felt a sticky substance all over my back.

Mother later found evidence of what had happened and had a heated argument with my dad. I was ordered to get into the bathtub and Mother came in looking very angry. She bathed me, cleaning me roughly and admonished me.

"We don't talk to anyone else about what happens in our house."

The incident was never mentioned again. I buried this event deep in my psyche. The only part I wanted to remember was that someone loved me.

Dad lavished me with praise and attention whenever he was around. Mother greatly resented any attention he gave me; no matter how abusive it was, thinking that it took attention away from her. I didn't understand her reaction to the molestation and felt totally abandoned. In an odd sort of way she seemed jealous of me.

Later that same night dad woke me and asked me to come into the living room. I remember that Mother was sitting on the couch and dad went over to a side chair. It was fairly dark in the room with only one light on. The drapes were pulled tight. Dad pointed me to another chair in the room. I sat down as instructed. I was uncertain and afraid of what was about to happen. It was obvious they had both been drinking and Mother seemed very angry. I sat in front of them both, shaking. I began crying.

Dad asked me which one of them I would like to live with. He reminded me how much he loved me and said he needed to see me more often. He was always nice to me and although I had experienced the rape, I felt his love whenever he was around. I suffered from Mother's constant criticism of everything I did, so I knew I really wanted to say I would prefer to live with him although obviously I knew very little about his life away from us. But I also knew that choosing him would be like slitting my own throat. I would not be able to endure Mother's wrath.

"I'll stay with Mother," I said through my tears.

I remember going back to bed and crying myself to sleep. I didn't understand all that had happened that day but was frightened of losing both parents. I knew that if I chose my dad over Mother, I would lose my mother's love, however inadequate. Yet, I knew that by choosing as I did, my father was lost to me forever. He left the next morning and I didn't see him for many years. The smell of stale alcohol still sickens me to this day.

Unloved and Unworthy

Early messages of shame clearly threatened my self-worth. Carol Christ writes "Because it is too painful, children attempt to suppress the primal experience of rejection. Rather than facing their past, unloved children come to believe that the world is an unloving place and that they are unworthy of love."[ii] Now we know we learn as children both from what we hear as well as what we see. Mother's constant criticism of me was painful. I was certain I was not loved by my own mother.

Because I was tall for my age and eventually towered over all the other kids in grade school, I felt awkward and was teased a lot. My eyesight was particularly bad in one eye and I suffered the humiliation of wearing a patch on my good eye to try to strengthen the weaker one. I had what's called "lazy eye" and it wandered wherever it wanted. Kids made fun of me. Because, as it turned out, I am legally blind in the weaker eye, I had a very difficult time functioning while wearing the patch. I would run into door frames and trip over things that I could not see. It was particularly awful.

In addition because I bit my fingernails, Mother would put awful tasting liquid on them. When that didn't do the trick, she made me wear white gloves to school. You can imagine how much fun other kids had with that, teasing me endlessly. The gloves didn't cure the situation either.

Mother's relentless demands kept me on my toes, ever fearful that I would make a stupid mistake. Much of the time I lived in sheer terror of her and what she could do to me. I remained cheerful on the outside, but inside I was crying most of the time. "...constant criticism [creates] a belief that love and approval come only to those who are perfect."[iii] Each day I tried to be perfect, but always found myself lacking. There seemed to be no escape.

I felt that my smile identified me; it was my trademark. I became so afraid to let my feelings show, everyone commented about my smile. It was plastered on and helped me get through each day. It became as much a part of me as my mantra of *Whatever I do is never good enough.* Even when I felt totally worthless, I had a smile on my face, however forced.

"[Children] suppress their feelings and sensations, the power of the life force within them, in their desperate attempts to please their parents. The price they pay is that they can no longer feel joy in their own lives."[iv] I tried to be a quiet, good little girl. I read a lot and stayed to myself. But my exuberance reappeared in school. I loved to talk to my classmates and frequently got into trouble for it. We were graded on how well we behaved in school, a report card entry included Deportment. The expectation was that we would be quiet and not talk to our classmates and pay attention in class. I was a daydreamer and often looked out the window. But how I did love to talk.

As I type these words I am reminded of how my perfectionism haunts me to this day. It has taken me years to finally write this book, afraid that I would not get it right.

The Un"Mother"ed Daughter

To note that Mother was cruel is rather an understatement. From the time I was a young girl she told me I had been an ugly baby. I internalized this as the "truth," lopped off the baby part, and lived for decades believing I was ugly. She also talked about how resentful she had been when she was pregnant with me. She was violently ill with morning sickness which could come on unexpectedly and not just in the mornings. She made it abundantly clear that I was a child who was not wanted.

I grew up hating my given name. Each time Mother wanted my immediate attention or I was in trouble, she called me my full name, Margaret Ruth. It became a symbol of anger and I shied away from wanting anyone to call me Margaret. Obviously I have to use in on legal paperwork, but I have even attempted to get my doctors' assistants to call me Margie. Sometimes they even remember. Still today I cringe when someone calls me Margaret.

At age 13 Mother decided I was fat. At that age, of course, I had not yet formed a waistline so she decided to put me in a girdle. This restrictive garment was meant to hold my stomach in. I wore it every day until I turned 18. Later I decided it was Mother's attempt at a chastity belt, keeping me safe from whatever might occur. And I internalized this comment as true – that I was fat. I also lived with that lie for many decades. It was true that I weighed more than my mother had as a teenager, but I was by no means fat. It was a trap to get me to comply.

I was constantly shamed and became worried about putting on weight. Even as I grew into a woman's body I still felt awkward with skinny legs and a straight up and down figure. The hourglass figures of models were not part of my existence. I became anorexic off and on for years.

As a child I was conflicted by my hatred of my mother. I don't really think now of having been "mothered," but that is exactly the point. Back then I firmly believed that Mother had driven my father away and I resented her for that.

"Children often fantasize about and idealize the absent parent, who is usually the father, and resent the caretaker parent, more frequently the mother."[v] This was certainly true in my case.

I fantasized about all the father-daughter banquets I never attended and blamed my mother. It seemed to be all her fault that dad was gone. I thought if Mother had only been nicer, he never would have left. She turned to her children to serve her every need: physical, emotional, sexual. "The ethos of domination and the poisonous pedagogy of control encourage parents and others to think that they are only doing what is expected when they abuse children."[vi]

Mother became an insatiable martyr, always telling us what she had sacrificed for us. Although it was true the divorce forced her to work to support her family, she liked to remind us that she never married again because of us. She threw her unhappiness in our faces and blamed all of life's burdens on having borne two children. She didn't take responsibility for her own choices, but blamed us for the choices she made. Since I was the energetic, boisterous child who looked just like my father, Mother seemed to resent me more. I resolved never to be like her.

> In her desire not to be anything like her mother, she may strive for power at the expense of other needs. The daughter flees the devouring mother who through her jealousy and envy of her daughter's talents and potential freedom, tried to imprison her. She distances herself from the mother who is overly judgmental, rigid and unsupportive. She shuns the martyr archetype of the mother who has sacrificed her own life to be of service to her spouse and children.[vii]

Mother instilled in us an incredible work ethic, but it came attached to the notion of trying to please her. I bristled under the conflicting feelings of working hard and needing to win her approval. It seemed that no matter what I did, it was wrong.

A carefree childhood seemed non-existent away from my grandparents. I was responsible for most of the ironing by the time I was 8. I even had to iron my brother's blue jeans! I started cooking family meals when I was 10. When I was 11 years old I was hired out to clean other people's houses. I recall Mother remarking that I would probably do a better job for someone else rather than for her. She knew she had trained me well in getting things clean. So since she was never satisfied with how I did things at home, she allowed me to clean for others. At least my "employers" praised me for doing a good job.

I found this experience leading me toward getting others to like me. That became critically important. I believed the way to do that was to do anything I was told, no matter how difficult and with a smile on my face. "I can't" was unacceptable. "Just do it" became the norm, long before Nike came along.

> Every depressed patient I have ever treated was a person who had lost his childhood. ... He had grown up too fast in an effort to meet expectations that were coupled with approval and acceptance. He had become or he had tried to become a doer and an achiever only to find that his achievement was meaningless, since it was at the expense of his being, now unable to be and unable to do, he falls into a depressive reaction.[viii]

I remember when I was a teenager and having the typical "asserting my independence" fights with Mother, she kept telling me I needed counseling. However, she said it shamefully and never did anything about seeking such help herself. Being in therapy still carried a stigma back then. If someone needed counseling they were derided as being weak or "crazy." Mother was not about to carry that burden too. It took a long time before mental health became as acceptable as seeing a doctor for physical reasons and still to this day it carries a stigma in the eyes of some.

Mother had a difficult time watching me grow up and become independent of her. I remember yelling at her once, saying that the more independent we became, as she had taught us on some levels to be, the more she fought it. She didn't like the fact that I had thoughts and opinions of my own that differed from hers. Like my grandmother I really cared about other people. Mother simply cared what others thought of us.

She claimed if I would live my life the way she thought I should live it, everything would be just fine. The only problem with that was there was no "I" separate from her. I was told I was selfish if I tried to stand up for my own beliefs. Our outlooks on life were drastically different and this was hard for her to accept. As a result I came to distrust my own thoughts and feelings which differed dramatically from things Mother believed.

Mother harbored racist thoughts which were largely a result of her growing up in Texas. She made no bones about that.

Her comments both embarrassed and offended me. I was captivated by Martin Luther King, Jr.'s speeches and wanted to take up his cause. I followed the Civil Rights activism with fervor. She had never trusted President John F. Kennedy, in part because he was Catholic, so when he was assassinated, Mother cheered. I was mortified. Her views were so disparate from my own it became another bone of contention.

As I got older Mother deeply resented the fact that I missed my grandmother and my father. It was years later that I realized I had probably expressed her grief for her as well as my own, crying myself to sleep each night. She seemed to find it impossible to outwardly grieve, believing that tears were a sign of weakness. Whenever there was loss in her life, she just shrugged her shoulders and moved on.

In hindsight I can see that she had no means of satisfying my yearnings for these significant individuals. There was nothing she could do to bring either back – but her instructions to "get over it" didn't satisfy me. I believe if she had ever acknowledged her own grief around her losses, we both would have been better off by sharing a common pain that might have led to deeper intimacy.

After I was married and had children of my own, Mother continued to insist that I serve her whenever and however I could. I worked full time, maintained my own house and family but still did all of her yard work and washed and set her hair three times a week. She said I owed it to her for all she had done for me. As she became more financially secure, she used money as a means to get me to do what she wanted. Whenever gifts were given, she retained ownership. Sometimes she would even ask for things back. Nothing came without a price.

When my husband and I decided to move away, Mother threatened to move along with us. She couldn't bear the thought of being left alone. She later commented that our leaving was harder on her than her divorce. She no longer had someone under her thumb to jump at her beck and call. She had to wait several more years until my niece and nephews grew up to have a new source of servants. However, they didn't respond in quite the same way.

> Many daughters experience a conflict
> between wanting a freer life than their
> mother and wanting their mother's love
> and approval. They want to move
> beyond their mother, yet fear risking the
> loss of their mother's love. Geographical
> separation may be the only way at first
> to resolve the tension between a
> daughter's need to grow up and her
> desire to please her mother.[ix]

My relationship with my mother greatly contributed to my lack of self-worth and my inability to say "no" to her demands. It contradicted everything inside me, but I strongly yearned for her approval and I remained tied. My mantra – *Whatever I do, it's never good enough* – actually had its origins in my childhood. My marriage became an extension of that life, so the mantra remained fixed for many years.

Patriarchy in Church and Family

"Patriarchal society has contempt for women, so the depressed woman hates herself."[x] The patriarchal environment in which I grew up and married into was fodder for my depression. Patriarchy is defined as a societal construct whereby the father is the leader of the clan and women and children are considered dependents. Males have ultimate power and control over everyone else.

Mother was as patriarchal as my grandfather. She wanted to be accepted in a man's world and believed that she needed to abandon her feminine self along with her intuition and feelings in order to find that acceptance. Mother often remarked that the greatest compliment she ever received was that she thought just like a man.

"The way to think abstractly is to define precisely, to create models in the mind and generalize from them. Such thought men have taught us, must be based on the exclusion of feelings."[xi]

Mother was incapable of passing along the nurturing qualities of a mother or the feminine mystique of a woman. She treated us like we were her property and told us to do only what she said.

Carol Christ tells us, "Denial of feelings is an important aspect of the Protestant ethic and the spirit of capitalism."[xii] My early church remembrances are of the Presbyterian Church in rural Minnesota. My mother rarely went with us, but my brother and I always attended both Sunday school and church. This was just expected of us but it was also something I enjoyed. I was confirmed at age 12. As I grew older I tired of the Presbyterian stewardship sermons – always asking for money for bigger and better church buildings. I don't remember hearing much about helping others or sending money for missionaries. I attended other churches occasionally with friends, but never on a regular basis.

****

I met my first real boyfriend when I was 15. My best friend had been dating him and decided she didn't want to see him anymore. She drove him over to my house and left him there. We began talking and enjoyed each other's intellect. He was older and had already started college.

Soon after we started dating I knew he was not a good match for me. He was very quiet and talked very little. I told him a few months later that I wanted to break up. He wrote me a letter saying that he would end his life if we weren't together. That was all it took. I was hooked. I couldn't bear the thought of having that on my conscience.

When we worked through all that, we attended the Church of Christ with other friends. We were baptized into the church together after we married. I was a faithful church-goer for several more years.

On a particular Sunday I heard the preacher call out the name of a parishioner and asked us all to pray for her because she was living in sin. I didn't believe a minister had the right to name someone publicly who had offended church teachings. I believe only God has the right to judge us. I swore on that day that I would never return to that church.

A few years later I decided to attend the Baptist church where my children went to day care. That fateful Sunday an evangelical minister was a guest preacher. It was there that I had a "born-again" experience. I had gone forward during the altar call and sobbed and sobbed as others surrounded me in support. I felt totally cleansed and released from self-inflicted bondage. Until that day I was drinking, sometimes heavily, and having an adulterous affair. Both ended abruptly, and I felt wonderful.

This experience was not greeted with congratulations from my husband or my mother. My husband, who was out of town that day, began to make fun of me upon his return and called me "Miss Goody Two-Shoes." My mother frequently had spoken out against

Baptists because when she was a girl she was not allowed to go on a field trip with her Sunday school class since she was not a member of that church. She never forgave the Baptists for that and blacklisted anyone who belonged to that denomination. It didn't take too long for my euphoria to come spiraling down. If my husband and my mother didn't approve, then I must be the one who was wrong.

The truth was that I had come from a dysfunctional background and married into another dysfunctional home. I didn't know how to maintain a sense of self. I suffered from low self-esteem and the only thing I could do well was work. I had been trained at an early age to place other people's needs before my own. What I thought or felt was never deemed very important and so I came to believe that my thoughts and feelings were secondary to everyone else's.

Matthew Fox describes this so well in his book *Original Blessing*. He writes about the effects of patriarchy and the concept of original sin on a person's psyche. "It divides and thereby conquers, pitting one's thoughts against one's feelings, one's body against one's spirit, one's political vocation against one's personal needs..."[xiii] I was unsure of who I was.

My husband benefited from this overarching commitment to please him. He was from Middle Eastern descent and had been taught that women were for pleasure and to cater to a man's every wish. He was the middle son of five boys and his mother's favorite.

He was used to having a special meal cooked just for him (his mother said he had special dietary needs), and having his clothes set out for him each morning.

Open marriage was popular at that time in the sexual revolution of the 1960s and he embraced that concept wholeheartedly. He teased about having a harem. He could not understand why I balked at having his girlfriend/secretary move in with us and share our bed. Since I held the belief that my mother should have been nicer to hold my father in the home, I put up with almost anything so he would never leave me. The only problem was that after a while I felt even more worthless and so disrespected in the relationship that I wanted him to leave!

Instead of being able to bring his girlfriend into our home, my husband began staying out at least one night a week. This became a trend that lasted many years. He found many other women who would accompany him to bed. I began to have irrational thoughts, wishing he would be killed some night when he was out, instead of facing the issue of divorce and believing that I was not able to do that. Emotionally I wasn't strong enough.

After our children were born, believing it was my responsibility to take care of them, my husband did not allow me to leave the house unless the children were asleep or I took them with me. He told me he would do nothing to help me around the house, so not to bother to ask. I took that to heart and did all the yard work, house repair, cleaning, tending the children and cooking meals. This was all in addition to working full time and responding to my mother's constant requests.

My husband went to work every day, but his spare time was spent reading and drinking. He wanted my full attention when he was at home and resented the time our children took away from him. I tried every trick I knew to please him and apologized for my every move. As with Mother, nothing seemed to work. The pattern was deeply ingrained in me. In fact later I had a job where I apologized so often my boss told me he would fire me if he heard me say I was "sorry" one more time. It seemed I apologized for my own existence.

I never really questioned male domination. It seemed a fact of life. It was all I had ever known. I wanted my children to have a father in the home so breaking free of my husband's control was counter to that. My mother had taught us to work hard but in her world men always came first. My brother was supposed to go to college while I was told to learn how to type. My older brother was clearly the favorite. He was quiet, reserved, and a male. He did not have the outgoing personality of our father. I did. Whenever Mother commented on how much I was like dad, she said it in such a tone that I felt ashamed. She would make comments about how I was just like him and then follow that with a comment about what a jerk he was. I thought she hated me as much as she hated him. She never talked about how much she loved him.

She remarked that my brother had been such a wonderful child because he was so quiet and played in the closet. Later I didn't have the heart to tell her that might not have been a good sign.

At times I resented being a female. As a child I was known as a tomboy, always climbing trees and playing in the dirt. I was chastised for getting dirty, but never praised for what I did well. I wanted to be accepted in a man's world too but, wishing to be different from my mother, I tried to make it by being nice. I quickly found that men frequently turned that into something sexual and I became rather promiscuous. After all, I had decided that my mother was cold and probably frigid, and this was one way I could prove that I was not like her.

Patriarchy, as I have come to understand, is also hard on males. They are not encouraged to express their feelings and when they do, they are often considered weak. If their feminine side is more prevalent, they may be outcast or bullied. They may grow up feeling that they are not good enough. They may seek power and control that is foreign to their way of thinking in order to be accepted. And they repress the very feelings that are part of them.

In the 1950s and 1960s men were expected to go to work and care for their families financially. Duties within the home were clearly divided. Women typically stayed home and raised the children. As the economy and society changed it became necessary for more and more women to work in order to make ends meet.

Men were suddenly expected to help with household chores and clashes in the home became more common. Women wanted them to change emotionally too. They expected clear communication and affection. Those changes did not come easily.

Big Changes

I had certainly encountered major changes in my own life. My dad's father, with whom we had lived, prepared to retire after 40 years. He had an 8th grade education and had moved up the ladder from errand boy to general manager. He and grandma decided they should move to Dallas, Texas, where their only daughter lived and the climate was less formidable. Winters were difficult in Minnesota and as he faced retired life grandpa longed for a little less snow plowing and a lot more sunshine. They traveled to Dallas and bought a house three doors down from my aunt. It was a lovely home and would suit them just fine. The day after the papers were all signed, grandma dropped dead of a heart attack, still in Dallas.

My favorite 8th grade teacher who was also our neighbor called me out of class to tell me. I was devastated. I knew then there was no one else who loved me. I felt totally alone.

I remember standing with my grandfather at the open casket prior to visitation and listening to him talk about how sorry he was that he had not been the best of husbands. He felt he had failed grandma in many ways. Later in the day Mother commented that it was probably wrong that he had shared all of that with me since I was still so young.

I remember clearly what I was wearing at Grandma's funeral: a knit patterned off-white dress and gray coat with black velvet collar. It was March, a slushy, messy month toward the end of a Minnesota winter. I felt invisible. We were to look good as always and not make a scene. Although I cried silently it was apparent that no one around me was concerned about how I was doing. All the adults seemed to think that children were too young to grieve or care about such things. But to me she was the most important person in the world, never to be forgotten.

In June of that same year, my brother (captain of the basketball team) and his girlfriend (one of the cheerleaders), found themselves needing to get married because of an unplanned pregnancy. They were both 16 and had a year to go before graduating from high school. This event caused quite a stir in the family to say the least.

Mother told me that the family (meaning her) was very embarrassed by this event. She felt it reflected poorly on her image as the perfect mother. I remember thinking how sad it was that she felt that way upon such a joyous occasion. She cautioned that I should never let the same thing happen to me. Through this event I also lost my brother, whom I idolized. Even though they lived with us for quite a while longer, I never got much attention from my brother after he married.

By August my grandfather had finished work and was preparing to move to his new home in Dallas. He convinced my mother that we should all accompany him. After all he was still very much the patriarch of the family. That way he could keep tabs on us and have us nearby. Mother bought a house, a foreclosure, a block away from Grandpa, and we were on our way. The trip took two full days and I remember lying in the back seat of the car the whole way either crying or sleeping. In my mind everything I had known as stable and secure was gone. Even my beloved piano didn't make the trip.

As luck would have it, dad was living in Dallas at this time. He and mother had reconnected at grandma's funeral and they spoke of remarriage. Mother insisted that dad get a job and support the family. He was an incredible charmer and could sell anything, but he had had a serious drinking problem since high school and had not held a steady job in years. Six weeks after we arrived in town, he married another woman, also an alcoholic.

Again, my mother was deeply hurt, but held it all together. She interviewed with a doctor, a urologist who was establishing a new private practice. The doctor's wife was a friend of my aunt's and introductions were made. Mother got hired and threw herself into learning medical terminology and procedures. Work became her salvation. I was left alone for long periods of time.

I ended up in a junior high school with 1500 kids. This was a complete culture shock after being in a school of about 200 kids in 12 grades. It was a complete reversal from rural life. These new classmates were wearing makeup and talking about sex, things I had never really thought of. I had just turned 14. It was a difficult transition to say the least. I remember being told that I would be accepted by the popular kids if I agreed to have sex with one of the football players. I was shocked.

After my brother and his young family moved away, Mother frequently stayed at work until 10 or 11 o'clock at night. When she got home she would expect me to have dinner ready for her and sit and talk about her day and how hard her life was. When I begged her not to work so much and spend more time with me, she accused me of being selfish and said she was just trying to support us. She needed to work to survive. "Many women have sacrificed too much of their souls in the name of achievement."[xiv]

My resentment of Mother deepened during this period and I longed for freedom from her. Because she was very embarrassed about my brother getting married young, she was overprotective of me. Limits were placed on my every move. With grandma gone there was no lifeline or connection to weekly church services. Mother was told she was not welcome in the local Presbyterian Church because she was divorced. I babysat frequently for my aunt and her friends. This was the only time I was away from home and did not yet have a social life. Within the first year of our move to Dallas, my medical ailments began to emerge. They always seemed to arise when I was babysitting.

Medical Conditions and Treatment

Shortly after we moved it seemed there was always something wrong with me. Often the doctors would shake their heads and say they had no idea what caused the problem. I don't recall anyone ever asking me how I felt – not just physically, but certainly not emotionally.

I began to suffer from chronic bronchitis. I coughed so loud that people would stop and stare. I was treated with an inhaler, cough syrup and antibiotics, but nothing seemed to completely eliminate the cough. I remember going to the doctor one day and he told my mother that I was merely crying out for attention. I was incensed! Little did I suspect it to be true. Mother chose to ignore me more than usual after that. She criticized me for having her take time off work to have the doctor diagnose something which was not "real." This cough stayed with me off and on for another ten years.

By the time I was nearly 15, I developed a swelling of my hands and feet. This usually occurred when I was babysitting and not in my own home. I would also break out in hives for no apparent reason. Numerous tests were run and it was finally determined after many months that I had rheumatoid arthritis. The doctor admitted that it was quite unusual for someone so young to have this diagnosis, but he couldn't figure anything else out. The only thing we were told to do was wait until the crippling began. Luckily it never did.

I desperately wanted to be free of my mother, and went through intense periods of despair and anger in my teens. The more I asserted my independence, the more restrictions were placed on me. I would lie in bed at night thinking of ways to kill her, but knowing I couldn't. I would never get away with it.

I was bored in high school and my first and only boyfriend (who would later become my husband) and I were limited in how much we could see each other or even talk on the phone. After a while we knew Mother would always be late coming home from work so he began coming to our house in the afternoon after I got home from school. He was four years older and by this time already in college. Because of the limits placed on how often we could see each other, our relationship became sexual very quickly. After our first sexual experience I remember sobbing for hours, but I didn't understand why. At that time I had no memory of the childhood molestation.

Six months after I graduated from high school, I got pregnant. We had used rhythm as a birth control method and it had worked for almost two years. My periods were like clockwork and I always knew when I was ovulating. I was highly attuned to my body and knew immediately when I became pregnant. We quickly began planning to get married. Mother was very upset and that is an understatement.

We had a small wedding in a local Baptist church. Family and friends joined us and I was later told that my father was sighted in the back of the church but left before I knew he was there.

By the time I got prenatal care, I was four months pregnant. My blood pressure was very high and the doctor figured that if my weight became too excessive my blood pressure would increase even more. I was placed on diet pills (amphetamines) to keep my weight down.

I loved being pregnant and felt more vital and fully alive than at any other time in my life. Midway through the third trimester my blood pressure rose to unsafe levels and the doctor decided to induce labor. I had gained only 14 pounds. I arrived at the hospital still very thin and not in labor. The nurses were incredulous when I told them I was there to have my baby. They refused to admit me as a patient until the doctor arrived.

The doctor came in, examined me and broke my water. I was immediately put to sleep with sodium pentothal. Within hours my blood pressure rose to 210/140 and the doctor informed my husband and my mother that I probably wouldn't make it. He expected me to go into convulsions which would strangle the baby. The doctor asked if he should try to save me or the baby. What a choice for a 22 year old prospective father to make!

Spirit was watching over me as always and both new mother and son made it through. Although I had been unconscious the entire time, my husband's arm was black and blue from me squeezing it during labor. I was kept heavily sedated in the hospital for only a few days before being ordered to go home to a week of complete bed rest.

Mother jumped in to take control. We moved into her house and she helped with the baby. Rather than expressing concern for my well-being, she just commented that it was good that the birth was induced so she could tell everyone the baby was premature. She was more concerned about what the neighbors thought than how I was. Other family members were told they could not hold the baby because she didn't want him to be spoiled. My blood pressure returned to near normal and I was released to go back to work within three weeks. Breast feeding was not considered an option since I needed to keep working. God blessed us richly and our son was a wonderful baby. He slept and ate and whenever he was awake, he was smiling.

The next few years were a blur of work, diapers, moving to our own house and more work. When our son was nine months old I suffered a rather severe, but delayed, postpartum depression. Although I was very unhappy in my marriage, I attributed it to how quiet my husband was, and blamed everything on his lack of support and assistance with chores.

I remember him walking into the kitchen one morning and finding me with a butcher knife pointed at my stomach. The thought of continuing to live while feeling so depressed was unthinkable. I don't recall the instance clearly, but I remember going to the doctor soon after and sitting on the exam table crying. The doctor prescribed some "happy" pills, antidepressants which merely numbed me and kept the smile on my face. There was never any discussion of whether or not the birth control pills, newly developed, could cause depression. The doctor simply wanted to know how my blood pressure was doing.

With so much responsibility and unhappiness in my marriage, I began looking for love in all the wrong places. My husband was already involved with other women by then, so I felt somehow it would be okay if I strayed from my marriage vows too. I had an affair with a man at work but felt guilty about it. It didn't fill the void in my life and fed my despair. Nothing I said or did seemed to please my husband or entice him to deeper intimacy. He never told me he loved me, and I interpreted this to mean he didn't. After all I believed I was unlovable. "Knowledge of who we are, independent of other people, is crucial to self-esteem."[xv] Thoughts of suicide permeated my life.

Like many other women I thought having another child might be the answer. I enjoyed being a mother and loved being pregnant. Taking care of a child in the dependent infant state was very gratifying. I knew the work involved in having one child; how could having another be any harder? I liked having a brother three years older than me, so I wanted to have a daughter around the time our son turned three. I had been on birth control pills for more than two years and the month I went off of them I became pregnant for the second time. Again, I knew the next morning that I was pregnant.

I sought care from the same physician who had delivered my son and he was prepared to watch the pregnancy carefully. I didn't take diet pills, didn't gain very much weight and my blood pressure remained a concern. Again I felt wonderful physically and excited to have another baby. Two weeks before the due date with my blood pressure on the rise, my doctor decided to induce labor because he didn't want delivery to interfere with his summer holiday weekend plans. A shot of Pitocin was administered in the doctor's office and the baby was delivered three hours later, luckily in the hospital delivery room. Although the doctor admitted later that he was afraid he would lose me again, the spiking of my blood pressure during labor was attributed to a simple kidney infection.

I was blessed with a baby girl and she was everything I ever hoped for. I cried with joy. Since my husband was one of five boys I had thought for sure I would have another boy. Having a daughter three years after our son was an unexpected miracle. I had always dreamed of recreating a wonderful relationship between big brother and little sister.

When our daughter was about three months old I began bleeding in between my monthly cycles. I had always had heavy bleeding with periods lasting 8-10 days.

"Chronically heavy periods can be related to chronic stress over second-chakra issues, including creativity, relationships, money, and control of others."[xvi]

This time the bleeding was rather light, but continuous and never went away. A few different brands of birth control pills were prescribed to see if they made any difference. They didn't. Over the next year I endured monthly pelvic exams, two D&C's (dilation and curettage of the uterine lining), cauterization of my cervix, hormone shots and frequent pap smears. Nothing seemed to work and I was miserable.

No one ever seemed to question that the first-generation birth control pills which were very strong could have caused any of my problems. I am convinced they were the culprit.

After 15 months of agony and no long term solutions, a hysterectomy was scheduled. I was 23 years old. I had told the doctor that unless something was done to control the bleeding, I would kill myself. I could not stand the stress any longer.

"Disease [in the sexual organs]" Northrup tells us, "is not created until a woman feels frustrated in her attempts to effect changes that she needs to make in her life."[xvii] I knew I was unhappy, but that was all I knew.

The abdominal surgery was performed and I became one minus a uterus. Shortly thereafter my incision was reopened to release a virulent staph infection. I was placed in isolation and remained in the hospital for ten days. I cleansed the hole in my abdomen for more than three weeks before it finally healed.

> The uterus is related energetically to a woman's innermost sense of self and her inner world. It is symbolic of her dreams and the selves to which she would like to give birth. Its state of health reflects her inner emotional reality and her belief in herself at the deepest level. The health of the uterus is at risk if a woman doesn't believe in herself or is excessively self-critical.[xviii]

Standard recuperation after this type of surgery was six weeks. Friends and neighbors assisted my husband and mother in keeping things running smoothly. My grandfather visited every day. I was unable to lift the children or even sit up for long periods of time. Amazingly, during this period my fingernails grew to a beautiful length. I had bitten my nails since I was a small child. Once people started listening to my needs instead of the other way around, I was under less stress and stopped biting my nails. That was a great insight at the time. Unfortunately it didn't take long for the stress to take over and my nails were gone again.

One year later I was back in the hospital. This time after hours of excruciating pain, an appendectomy was ordered. When I came out of the anesthesia, the doctor told me there was nothing wrong with my appendix but he removed it anyway. My ovary had been bleeding into the abdominal cavity. He left that alone. No alternatives to surgery had been discussed.

> Allopathic medicine uses surgery, chemicals, or radiation to aggressively combat whatever ails the body, while alternative medicine tends to focus on helping the body heal itself, by nutrition, restoring balance, ridding itself of toxins, and engaging the mind and spirit in the process.[xix]

Sometime after this I ruptured a disc in my lower back. According to Louise Hay, back issues are caused by lack of support. And unsupported was exactly how I felt. I was so confused by all my medical issues I hardly knew what to do. I was increasingly depressed. My body was now badly scarred along with stretch marks from my pregnancies and I certainly didn't feel attractive. I kept looking for reassurance from someone – anyone – that I was okay. I pursued relationships with other men, some lasting several years. I became active in political causes. Any attention I got didn't get me anywhere positive. I threw my life into work since that was all I knew.

Finding My Way

Away from my mother's constant overbearance, I still never felt the freedom I so craved. I found out later it was freedom within I was seeking, but I didn't know that at the time. Anna Freud tells us "I was always looking outside myself for strength and confidence but it comes from within; it is there all the time." I suffered severe headaches every evening on the ride home from work. My husband and I worked near each other and always carpooled together. We frequently joined each other for lunch too, since he wanted to know what I was doing all the time. He actually was my best friend then, just not the best choice for a husband. We had an inexplicable bond.

I wanted more – much more – than he was able to give. I never believed he loved me. He never said those words and had steady girlfriends. About once a year I would ask for a divorce. He would treat me better for about three weeks and help around the house. He would clear the table and pick up clutter in the family room. He even helped with the dishes. He paid more attention to me. Then we'd be back where we started. He told me spending time with him was more important than a clean house; but he also wanted me to cook a dinner meal especially for him, just like his mother had done. She had spoiled him with whatever he wanted to eat and lots of times didn't bother to cook for anyone else. He agreed with the notion that children should be seen and not heard and he didn't interact with them much. I spent as much time with my kids as I could outside of work to make up for the fact that I was gone all day, but they were always put to bed early to please my husband.

My life included the wonderful children I wanted, spaced just properly, but otherwise I was unhappy most of the time. I enjoyed the different jobs I had but they did not challenge me mentally. My health, as noted before, was up and down. My blood pressure dropped significantly after the hysterectomy and I was not on medication.

My friends and family all said I was intuitive and could accurately predict things that would happen. I listened to my intuition, but I was no longer in tune with my body. ". . . dualistic habits of thought have led many to discount feeling and sensation as less important than thinking."[xx] I relied on inner promptings when I felt them, but became more disassociated from my body. Every day became a blur.

I went through the motions of mundane life, always went to work even when I didn't feel like it, and found someone else to care for my children. When I would beg to stay home with the kids, my husband convinced me that we needed the income from my employment. It was really needed to buy his books and booze and cigarettes, but I didn't challenge him. In fact, at times I would be the one to get a second job to supplement our income. One summer I worked the graveyard shift at the local cannery working with beets and corn. I would come home covered in pink juice, sticky. The smell of fresh beets stuck with me for a long time. I was still working all day at my regular job. Needless to say I was exhausted.

Our move to Oregon had come through my intuition. We traveled there on a short vacation and while driving home, I said I thought we were supposed to live there. I believed I had been given a clear message that was where we belonged. I had had my "born-again" experience a year or so before and trusted that this was in God's plan for us. At the end of our vacation, we put the house up for sale and the first people who looked at it decided to buy it. We were excited to be on our way. I just knew this would offer the freedom I still craved.

When our parents asked where we were headed, we responded "Oregon."

"But where in Oregon?"

"We don't know. We just know that is where we are supposed to live. We will figure it out when we get there."

Obviously they thought we were crazy. We took our young children out of school and set out on our new adventure. We soon arrived in the state capital and eventually my husband worked for the state while I went to work in the state legislature. I worked for a member of the House of Representatives and began watching the representative in the area where we lived. I decided that I could do a better job and began setting the stage to run against this fifth generation farmer. I had lived in Oregon for two years and resided in a mobile home. His family had been in the area for generations. There was an obvious bias against me because I didn't have those credentials. It didn't help that I was a woman running for office in the 1970s when that still was not a frequent occurrence.

I circulated a petition to get my name on the ballot. This way I could avoid paying the filing fee. Through this process I found many people excited about my involvement. It didn't take very long before I had enough signatures. These were turned in to the Secretary of State and I was on my way.

To establish local ties and credentials I joined the local planning commission and was elected to the school board where my children attended school. I campaigned hard and found it was exhilarating. I went door to door all over the district and met lots of wonderful people. Most of them said they had never met anyone running for office. I heard that my opponent was quoted as saying "everywhere I go she has already been." I went to town hall meetings, coffees in people's homes and met with people who gathered in local restaurants. I enlisted the help of several volunteers, but did much of the work myself. By the end of the campaign I had driven over 10,000 miles in six months.

On election night we stayed home to follow the returns. I lost by a relatively small margin and was heartbroken. My mother had come to Oregon for the election and told me "chin up." I stuffed all of my feelings and wrote it off as a good learning experience. I never ran for public office again.

Shortly after the election we decided to buy a small farm and I was hired in the state Senate on a permanent basis. We grew most of our own food and it all seemed idyllic. I would milk the goats before leaving for work and then again in the evening. My daughter helped me with feeding and cleaning the pens. She kept the house clean and helped with meals. Our son took care of most of the other animals and my husband took up gardening. However, I was so frazzled with all the work and outside activities that I collapsed. I resigned from the school board and said goodbye to the planning commission. I was running scared and didn't know where to turn.

First, my back went out again. The herniated disc from years before frequently caused me pain. One of my ankles started swelling every day. I was under a great deal of stress. The doctor prescribed exercises for my back and decided to operate on my ankle to remove the fluid he suspected was in the myelin sheath. There wasn't any there and he never figured out what the problem was. It was chalked up to arthritis. Six weeks later I dislocated my knee cap on the other leg. I was confined to a wheelchair at work which said on the back "Psychiatric Security Review Board." I felt that was where I really needed to be - in the psych ward. My co-workers fondly teased me about the words on the borrowed wheelchair.

About the same time all this was happening in my body, our house was broken into six times in seven months. We eventually caught the neighbor boy jumping over the fence as we arrived home from work. He was looking for alcohol and money. He destroyed many precious belongings including the hand painted Christmas ornaments that had been my grandmother's.

This time, knowing who was breaking into the house, I was more than just afraid. I feared for the safety of my children. My daughter would come home from school by herself, walking by their house as she got off the school bus. She would hide behind a chair when she was alone, afraid that the intruder would again come in. I had no idea what he would do if he found her. I feared for our lives living near these neighbors. And I feared my husband and his anger. He was drinking heavily in those days and had bought a gun for protection. Guns scared me, especially in the hands of an inebriated man. I declared I could not live there any longer. Our marriage was on the rocks and we abandoned our small farm and the dreams it held. All I could think about was suicide as a way to lessen the anguish. These thoughts were with me every day.

When I went in for a regular checkup of my blood pressure, my doctor quickly found out about my mental state as I began crying. He gave me two names and phone numbers. I was instructed to call one of these psychiatrists within three days or he would put me in the hospital. I didn't want to see the inside of a hospital ever again and I hesitatingly phoned the female psychiatrist. This was the first step on a long path toward wholeness.

> In general, people who go into therapy are
> outwardly healthy – one would never
> characterize them as 'sick.' Nevertheless,
> such people are the bearers of serious inner
> conflicts that can paralyze their lives, while
> their private suffering is still scarcely visible
> to the outside world.[xxi]

I was placed on small dosages of an antidepressant, which worked on the chemical imbalance in the brain. The doctor told me if I could continue to go to work each day and see her once a week, I would get better faster. She asked me to tell her about my needs but I had no idea what they were. When asked what I liked to do, I had no response. "Traumatized by disconnection, we distance ourselves from the pain through dissociation; alienated from our own feelings, we become all the more incapable of forming authentic connection.[xxii]

I managed to show up at work even though many times a day I would burst into tears, seemingly for no reason. All I could do was go through the motions of life. Days and nights seemed endless. The pills made me sleep, but I was restless in bed and out. My life as I knew it was crumbling. When I complained about my husband's alcohol consumption (two martinis before dinner and a six pack of beer after), he told me it was my problem. I had no idea who I was outside of marriage, but I knew I needed to get out. I was terrified and my smile had left me.

We ended up moving into town and bought another house while I wrestled with what to do. I had known this man since I was 15 years old and the thought of breaking up the marriage was still an anathema to me. I knew I would not survive if I stayed so I gathered my strength. I no longer worried about whether or not he would commit suicide without me in his life. I just knew I was on the verge of it myself.

In 1984 a few days after we finally separated, I was out in the yard pruning and trimming, trimming and pruning. I was trying to get the house ready to sell and we had an acre and a half of lawn, shrubs and flower beds to tend. Backyard burning was legal at that time and I formed a large pile of brush. I poured liquid all over it, stood next to the pile and lit a match. It wasn't until later that I realized I had used gasoline rather than something less flammable. The fire burst up in my face and I had the presence of mind to turn and roll in the grass. Neighbors heard me scream and came running. They got me into a car and took me directly to the hospital. Someone hosed down the fire until it went out. My daughter was left alone, not knowing what would happen to me.

I spent the next week in the hospital. The pain was excruciating as my arms were soaked in Betadine and the skin brushed off with a metal brush. My face was covered in gauze and cream since I couldn't very well soak it in a tub of medicine. My lips swelled up until I could see them below my nose. I lost all the skin on my face, arms and hands. My glasses saved my eyes. This was the worst pain I have ever experienced.

I mention this event mostly because of my husband's reaction. He had gone out of town that day and was notified I was in the hospital. When he called to see if I wanted him to come back and take care of me, he told me God was punishing me because I was ending the marriage. I did not agree and told him I could make it on my own. I knew if I let him come back, I would never again be free. This was a major turning point in my life. I began to reclaim my Self and slowly discover the person I had become.

A Paradigm Shift

I spent the next few years in therapy, wrestling with my past, with my relationship with my mother, with feelings of abandonment. I finally separated emotionally from my husband. My mother's reaction to the separation was "How can you do that – after all I've done for you?" She barely spoke to me for the next year. By now the children were almost grown and I could avoid the feelings of denying them a father figure in the house. Years later I was able to talk with the kids about how their father was actually absent although his body showed up at home almost every day. I apologized to them for my mistakes.

These were not easy conversations. I felt I had done many things wrong. But my heart was always in the right place. I loved my children and wanted only the best for them. We can only work with what we know and I explained that to them. I felt they understood what I was trying to say through my tears. Forgiving myself was another matter left to another time.

Digging into all the dark places of my life was very painful. The therapist encouraged me to look at the positive things I had gotten from my mother. I didn't want to. I wanted to continue hating her and blaming her for all of my unhappiness. It was because of her that I had stayed in a miserable marriage for so many years. It was because of her that I didn't have a father. It was because of her that I felt like shit.

My thoughts of suicide continued, often emerging several times a day. I thought of all the different ways I could end my life, but then I would think of my daughter and my son and how much I loved them. What would this do to them? If I were gone they would be left in the care of their inattentive father or my mother. These were untenable choices. I found I could bear my own pain more easily than thinking about theirs. However, just getting through the motions of each day took a lot of effort.

After several months I decided to take a night class at the local community college and encountered a wonderful philosophy teacher. That first semester she talked about Kepler and the universe, about things I had only dreamed of. I was hooked and this became my new lifeline.

This instructor became my neighbor when I rented the house across the street from her. We had numerous conversations each week. She became my first true mentor since my grandmother's death. She encouraged me to think and affirmed that I was a bright student. She was in the habit of writing long responses to her student's papers. These comments were offered as a way of opening up other perspectives. I felt a new sense of validation. "Self-expression is another basic need of all human beings and of all creatures. The need for self-expression underlies all creative activity and is the source of our greatest pleasure."[xxiii] After completing all the available philosophy classes and taking two years of a foreign language at the community college level, I was prepared for bigger and better things. This instructor and neighbor was a part of my life for many years to come.

I quit my job at the legislature and went to work in the government affairs office at the University of Oregon. I enrolled in school and looked forward to a new life. My soon to be ex-husband (three years after we first separated) told me that women who go to college later in life always end up divorced. If I'd known that was all it took, I would have started sooner! My daughter and I were in freshman biology together and I began to dream of someday having a college degree. Maybe that would prove I was worthy.

Mother, still angry about the breakup of my marriage, criticized me for changing jobs again. She asked me why I couldn't be more like my brother who had held a job for 25 years. I loved the challenge of learning new things and working in new environments. I could never be happy doing the same thing over and over again. Since she believed that women did not need a college education, she chastised me for that choice too. I tried to ignore her continuous disparagement. When I graduated a few years later, she didn't attend. I was hurt but also glad she wasn't there.

Clearly I knew how to juggle a lot of balls in the air. I took a full load of classes at school, worked myself up to director of the department and did some grant writing for professors and non-profit groups on the side. A friend told me of a small non-profit sexual abuse agency that was looking for a fundraiser/grant writer. I was quickly embraced by the directors and group leaders. The agency was dysfunctional and I was a great co-dependent helper. Whatever needed doing, I volunteered. My days were busy with school and my nights were devoted to volunteering.

When I began volunteering with them, they requested that I attend their 16-week group so that I would understand exactly what they did. While attending my first group, we were each asked to tell our story of the abuse we had endured. I talked about a difficult childhood with memories of physical and mental abuse. I had not yet accessed the memories that would come of what else had happened to me.

One of the women began talking about the enemas she had endured as a child. It was referred to as a form of sexual violation. I recalled the countless times we had been subjected to enemas. Mother said they were another way to get completely clean. She would take each of us into the bathroom and begin injecting warm water into our rectums. This happened every few weeks for several years. Mother also frequently gave herself an enema. Upon hearing the other woman's story, I began sobbing. It took me a full hour after group ended before I could pull myself together. The dam had been broken and pain poured out. Memories began flooding back.

Luckily school kept me sane. I loved the academic setting and was hungry to learn as much as I could about anything and everything.

> The world of scholarship is one of these magic circles that many of us slip into at regular intervals and bring everything we've thought we thought into question, and it can feel timeless and freeing – even magical.[xxiv]

My spontaneity returned at the urging of other students and quite often I felt happy. I was promoted at work and began lobbying and doing governmental relations work for all of public higher education in Oregon. I found another wonderful counselor and entered therapy on a regular basis.

I met a man who was working at the sexual abuse agency and whenever I showed up there, he would give me a hug. He was someone who was very warm and gentle and understanding of my emotional upheaval. After several months of dating, we moved in together. Mother called to say she didn't approve. She didn't think I should be living with someone if we weren't married. I thanked her for sharing and reminded her I was 40 years old and didn't need her approval. But of course, I wanted it. I hadn't yet reached the forgiveness stage that provided my healing.

Healing Through Faith and Spirituality

I still had a long way to go before I felt free. "What we create in the world, we must first create within ourselves. For there to be magic in your life, you must first believe in magic."[xxv] The next few years were magical, filled with great learnings both personal and intellectual. My new man, who within a year became my husband, helped me in many ways. He talked, he listened. He made me feel safe, an important feat in such a tumultuous time. He cooked dinner. He did dishes. He waited patiently while I finished my homework. And he loved me. Ironically, he never told me he loved me except on our wedding day. But I knew he did. It was something that sunk in. I understood it at my core. And it was wonderful. I expected it to last forever.

I had begun attending personal growth and development workshops which enabled me to see things with more clarity. There was talk of living as your word, authenticity and integrity, things that resonated in me. My career was also taking off as I became the Executive Assistant to a College President. Everything was clicking for me.

However, my new husband was not on the same path. He didn't have a steady job after the sexual abuse agency stint ended and became uncertain how to deal with things. He struggled with self-doubt and his own self-worth issues. On our second anniversary, he told me he would like to begin seeing a woman that he had dated previously. He wanted my approval. He was taking her out to lunch one day and concerned about what he should wear.

I remember screaming at him "I'm your fucking wife for Pete's sake. I don't care what you wear."

Soon after he decided to leave me and move in with Ann.

I remember telling him, "Perhaps we've learned what we came into each other's lives to learn."

He loved that phrase and repeated it frequently to our friends.

"What Margie said made so much sense." I began to cringe every time I heard the phrase again. Although I believed it in my core, it went against my vows of marriage.

After moving out he wasn't in touch for quite a while. After about six months he showed up at my door and said he had made a mistake. He asked if he could come back. I wasn't willing to have another husband who "entertained" other women, and we parted after some more expletive-filled comments from me.

It was at this point that I began to grieve. I grieved the end of my first marriage, which I had not done before because of the sense of release from bondage I had felt. I grieved my childhood and all that went with it. And I grieved the loss of this, my second marriage. All these losses threw me back into my unlovable, unworthy sense of self. I knew I needed help and this time I turned to God.

My spiritual journey became very eclectic. I wanted to know everything about every religion and tradition. Labels didn't matter to me and I didn't concern myself about the teachings as much as how I felt in a particular house of worship. I was also a student of astrology and Tarot. I was what everyone called a "seeker."

I walked down the street to attend the local Baptist church. After all I still considered myself a Baptist. My intuition had been prompting me that I belonged at the Nazarene Church which was closer to home. That day the service at the Baptist church was so awful I almost walked out. Everything the minister uttered I seemed to disagree with. So the next Sunday I obeyed my inner guidance and attended Nazarene services. I felt as if I had come home.

I knew very little about the Nazarene denomination but I felt surrounded by love in this congregation. I soon became a faithful attendee although I found the teachings less liberal than my core beliefs. It was good to be back in the ritual of a church service. The minister was a great preacher and I was grateful to take communion again. It wasn't long before I was attending church three times a week and involved in church activities such as feeding and housing the homeless.

Vicki, the Associate Minister befriended me. She would come to my house at least once a week and have tea. She listened to my deep pain and grief. She gave me a deeper sense of God and my relationship to that Divine Being.

I also began training as a Stephen's Minister, a non-denominational lay ministry designed to train congregants to assist others who were experiencing trauma or grief. I had a lot of experience with both and embraced the teachings with an open heart. Little by little I became more grounded and sure of myself. I was soon paired with a young woman who needed a lot of guidance.

I met with Julie each week and we would sit and talk for hours. She was very unsure of herself and I am certain I learned as much from her as she did from me. I had a good listening ear and offered whatever support I could.

Not being one to sit still for long, it soon became time for me to move on. I had physically moved every two or three years since I left Texas, about 19 years before. I decided to move to California to get away from the rain in the northwest and take time to seek the self I wanted to be, away from everything familiar. I joined a group called *In Spirit* and spent a year meeting bimonthly with 17 other like-minded people, honoring the Divine and ourselves. It was a rich experience and I began to appreciate how the Divine had followed me or guided me at every turn. I let go of deep pain and allowed this group to nurture me. I learned how to *Be* instead of *Do*. It was a healing experience to be surrounded by people who acknowledged and embraced the growth and pain of our childhoods and together we moved to new levels of forgiveness and acceptance.

I soon got a job traveling around the state marketing technology seminars for local Chambers of Commerce and for Microsoft. I moved 19 times in 26 months. Having no roots or home base took its toll on my psyche, but I was free of responsibility except for myself. I worked hard and was my own boss most of the time. I began to establish a clearer image of myself and found things I enjoyed and discovered what nurtured me. I listened to what my body needed and heeded the callings of my soul.

I began to study the teachings of Emerson and Ernest Holmes, early leaders of Science of Mind and Religious Science churches. I looked at how my life was driven by a need to please others and succeed – whatever that meant. within me; in fact, was me.

In her book *Love and Power*, Lynn Andrews quotes Andrew Harvey's retelling of Rumi:

> I thought I had exhausted terror,
> being trampled
> To become Your dust, finer and finer
> . . .
> Then the night came when You
> whispered 'I am You'
> And vanished, leaving me
> everywhere nowhere.[xxvi]

I was actually lost in this new-found freedom. I could see the Divine in everything and everyone else, but had a hard time with the idea that God was in me too. I felt I wasn't good enough for that to be so and I had a lot of evidence to prove it. I had always felt unworthy. Having had two husbands who chose other women over me robbed me of every shred of self-worth. I sobbed for hours as the concept of God in me began to sink in and find my heart. The layers of the onion began to peel back.

Within a year of accepting the traveling job, I was diagnosed with diabetes at critical levels. My blood pressure was very high again and I had bouts of blurred vision and fuzzy thinking. The company I worked for went bankrupt soon after. I was despondent and felt I had nowhere to turn. I found myself at my son's door, jobless, penniless and in poor health. He and his second wife of one month took me in and old thoughts washed over me. Suicide tempted me. I felt like a 50-year-old failure. This time I decided to *will* myself to die. It took less energy and far less action.

I spent the next year sleeping, eating and spending time with my grandchildren. They alternated weeks with my son and their mother. I managed to do little more than housework and laundry.

> Women who have experienced a deep wounding in relationship to their mothers often seek their healing in the experience of the ordinary. For many this takes the form of *divine ordinariness*, seeing the sacred in each ordinary act, whether it be washing the dishes, cleaning the toilet, or weeding the garden. Woman is nurtured and healed by grounding herself in the ordinary.[xxvii]

I found I enjoyed these mundane tasks, but I questioned who I was outside of the work world. I was continually learning how to "be" and not "do." I immersed myself in silence, sort of a self-pregnancy. I was trying to learn to appreciate each moment without looking to the past or to the future for clues to my existence. I moved out to an extra room in my son's shop so the children could have separate bedrooms. I was isolated with no windows or regular doors. Basically I was just waiting to die. It was a very difficult time.

For many years I had had the feeling that no one would miss me if I was gone. It was one of the delusions that came along with thoughts of suicide. During this period of living with my son and his family, I discovered that I was loved. I was told by both my children how much I was missed when I was away. People seemed to care about what I thought and how I felt. I was humbled and grateful for their love and care. It was quite a revelation.

One day I went to church and heard the pastor say there was nothing we could do, no task we could accomplish, no good deed we could perform in order to deserve God's love more than it was available to us right Now. Nothing else needed to be added. I heard this message in a new way and decided that I wanted to accept that love and surrender all God required of me. I made a conscious decision to begin to live again.

It was clear to me that Spirit had guided my path for a very long time. I decided to surrender to what I believed God had been trying to tell me for years. I had been called to the ministry in my late 20's, but always responded that I wasn't good enough. I didn't know enough yet. Although I never stopped believing in God, I had not embraced the promptings I frequently heard. I finally heard God's words to me that I was exactly what was wanted. After all, this wasn't about ME. It was about sharing love and the Divine.

My body was still on a downward spiral however. It hadn't caught up to my new beliefs. I began working again and my energy levels improved. But then one day I had a severe migraine headache in the back of my skull. I had never experienced such horrific pain in my head. Along with the headache all of a sudden the left side of my body wasn't working very well. I couldn't walk normally and could no longer put my left arm behind my back to fasten my bra. I wasn't sure what was happening. Now what was I going to do?

PART II

A New Life

The next day I went to Urgent Care and described my symptoms. I was told that it was probably large muscle nerve neuropathy caused by diabetes. The doctor suggested I see a physician in my local small town. I walked away feeling that the diagnosis was probably inaccurate but having nothing else to go on, I called to make an appointment with the recommended doctor. I was told that I would have to wait a month to see her because she was on vacation.

I continued to go to work, dragging my left leg around like a pile of sand. It held me up but wasn't very stable. My balance was pretty off. I could still walk and talk but had little use of my left arm.

Upon seeing the new physician she listened to my neck with her stethoscope and immediately ordered an ultrasound. As I lay on the table the technician took what seemed an inordinate length of time and I began to be concerned. When she told me to stay right there while she consulted with my doctor, alarm bells began to go off in my head. After a few minutes I was instructed to return to my doctor's office, luckily in the same building.

The doctor informed me that I needed emergency surgery. She indicated I had probably had a stroke, confirming my thoughts of an earlier misdiagnosis. I began to cry. I was terrified. I remember calling my daughter-in-law from the front desk of the hospital building since I did not yet have a cell phone. I stood there sobbing, telling her that they were going to keep me and I wouldn't be coming home that day.

The ordeal began with an angiogram while I listened to country music. The technicians laughed and talked among themselves. I felt very disconnected from my body but was asking questions. Later the technician came and told me that he didn't usually let patients see their scans but I seemed interested. On the left side my carotid artery looked like my baby finger, fully open and wide. On the right side, however, there was just the tiniest length of thread open. I was horrified.

I lay on the gurney prior to surgery and told God that I would do whatever was asked of me. I remember waking up in the ICU with my daughter and daughter-in-law sitting on the floor in the corner. Nurse Polly was very irritated they were there and made that perfectly clear. However, they ignored her comments and stayed right there by my side but out of the way. It was quite a trying time for us all.

The vascular surgeon later told me I would not have lived another six months if the blockage had gone undetected. I had faced death squarely in the eye and again declared my intention to live. I prayed that I would be carried through this time and would resume my life with a stronger sense of faith and purpose. I had been confronted with my own mortality – and my own divinity.

Luckily the stroke was mild and the surgery created an amazing recovery. My daughter commented, "It's amazing what blood flow to the brain will do!" The physician suggested that I do whatever I could to eliminate stress from my life. I decided to quit my job much to the chagrin of my boss. I had been under constant pressure to perform at high levels since I was in sales. I had been one of the stars in the office.

After several months of recovery I moved away from family. Although my son assured me that he and his wife would welcome me to stay with them for the rest of my life, I craved my own independence.

I moved a short distance away and rented a room from a friend. She also had another house guest who talked about a university where they taught Art as Meditation and other interesting courses. It sounded like the perfect place for my daughter to get her Master's degree. She is very creative and I thought that sounded wonderful. That night when I went to bed a loud voice in my head said "No. This one is for you."

I researched the university online and immediately upon contacting the school, I knew that was where I belonged and the timing was right. When I first contacted them, it was early August with classes to begin on August 31.

"Well I'm sure I can't get in this fall because it starts so soon."

"Oh no, as soon as we get your application we can get you in."

"Well, I don't have any money, so I'm sure I won't be able to attend."

"No. You can apply for financial aid when you get here and then pay us when it shows up. Everything will be just fine."

Clearly, Spirit was in control of this one. So with a lump in my throat and excitement and anxiety filling me along with faith and trust, I said goodbye to family and friends and uprooted again for the sun of California. I had $500 to my name. It was five months after the life-saving surgery.

When I arrived for the first week's intensive training, I met a woman from Chicago who was interesting and fun. At the end of the week she decided to leave the program and return home. She offered me the room she had rented and her new phone number. The rent was paid for the first month which she also gifted me.

In studying at the University of Creation Spirituality (an ancient pre-Christ religious tradition) I discovered a new spiritual language and a new connection to the Divine through creativity and wonder. I began to express myself through poetry and art. I found a world outside of patriarchy. In the *Heroine's Journey*, Murdock tells a story similar to my own. "In my early years I identified the feminine as smothering and dangerous."[xxviii] At UCS I discovered a new sense of the sacred through teachings on Buddhism and Judaism, the Goddess tradition and a reconnection to the earth.

> When the sacred feminine can take root and bloom, everything that patriarchy has put aside blooms with it; inclusiveness, for example, in place of obsessive separations; laughter in place of solemnity. Painstakingly drawn lines of authority give way to creative partnerships, and everything that has been frozen thaws and flows and dances.[xxix]

In Creation Spirituality there are four distinct parts: the Via (read the Way of) Positiva, Via Negativa, Via Creativa and Via Transformitiva. I reached a new understanding of the Via Negativa – the time of darkness and despair had also provided a time of letting go. I let go of feelings of self-hatred and thoughts of self-destruction. I found the Divine in the darkness waiting for me to wake up – patiently waiting for me to remember.

> In Letting Be we learn to let others be. To let God be. And, perhaps, most basic of all, to let ourselves be. And to be with ourselves.

To befriend ourselves, as healthy solitude requires. We begin to learn our own holiness and goodness and then we are more fully prepared to welcome holiness and goodness in others without jealousy or recrimination. That is how deeply one is changed by learning to Let Be.[xxx]

I began to honor and appreciate all that I had been through and to acknowledge that each event had contributed to who I am today. I had experienced many "dark nights of the soul," and they had strengthened me. Rather than berating myself for different choices I had made, I engaged a new level of forgiveness. I awakened to how much I had been blessed in my life.

After graduation I moved back to Oregon to live at my son's. He and his wife had lost a newborn while I was in school and I wanted fervently to offer my support. It had been a very devastating time for the family. Within several months my daughter-in-law was pregnant again and ordered on strict bed rest for the duration of the pregnancy.

We spent days and days together, talking, sharing and laughing. She has a wicked wit and we laughed while laying on opposing couches in the living room. I drove her to doctor's appointments and we waited anxiously for test results. The pregnancy was definitely high risk. My grandson decided to arrive a few months early and was born with a perforated colon. After a month or so in the neonatal unit he was able to come home with a colostomy bag. We were all so grateful that he had survived.

I began to get restless and wanting to decide where my next journey would take me. As soon as my grandson was no longer seriously ill and he had healed from the second surgery to remove the colostomy bag, I began looking at chaplain training programs. I knew that I wanted to work with patients since I had been through a lot of hospitalizations and surgeries and intimately knew the fear that arises in the unknown. All the training programs in Oregon did not offer the benefits I needed or suit my interests. So again I began to look to California.

I soon found a hospital that offered a chaplain training program and had everything I needed. I applied and found that a woman who had graduated with me from UCS would be my supervisor. I looked forward to having a familiar face in my new surroundings. I had applied to begin in September and then got a call that they had an opening in June. It again felt like my path was clear and I was being led.

Upon arrival at the hospital I met the staff and was assigned to the Intensive Care Unit as my first rotation. This was known to be one of the most difficult assignments. There I found that the priest who had been on staff the longest would be my mentor. He was a kind, gentle man whose first instruction was to call him by name. He clearly wanted to be known as a regular guy and fellow chaplain rather than "Father." We joked and laughed and built an easy camaraderie.

I loved working with the ICU patients. Many of them were on respirators to assist their breathing and could not talk, but I made clear eye contact and we were able to communicate in a myriad of ways. One of my patients told another chaplain, "You know that chaplain with the blue eyes? She can see into your soul."

I grew close to the nurses and doctors who worked there. The hospital was a training hospital which meant many doctors were in residency programs and still learning. I remember one female resident who had been in medical school and in training with her son who was also studying to be a doctor. She was vibrant and caring and listened attentively to her patients. She fell into my arms crying one afternoon after losing three patients that day. As her tears fell she told me she didn't think she would be a very good physician if all her patients died. I listened and comforted her, assuring her that she was going to make a remarkable doctor. I knew the events of that day would strengthen her resolve and enlighten her learning.

The chaplain training program was one year long and divided into quarters. There were ten of us students in each quarter. Since I started in June I came in at the end of the year for one group and a new group joined me in September. The day was broken up by classes in the morning and ministering to patients in the afternoons. We learned a lot about each other as students and about our backgrounds. We each had studied different faith traditions and how to minister to a very diverse population. We were challenged by the program to be truthful in our interactions and to confront each other as well as our patients when appropriate. We worked with the concept of different reactions to illness such as blaming God or blaming oneself for their debilities. We also had to write spiritual assessments on each of our patients.

There were times during the training that I felt ill-prepared to be there. Most of my other colleagues had Master's degrees in Divinity from Christian seminaries. My Master's degree was in an alternative religion. It took a lot of coaching from supervisors and lots of tears to truly believe in myself. I was an excellent chaplain in terms of patient interactions, but somehow felt incompetent among my peers. I had not studied the same types of things they had. I was not a Bible scholar. I was not a lot of things I perceived the other students were. But I knew how to be with people who were ill or dying.

One day after I had been at the hospital for about six months, the priest I worked with – I will call him Dan - ended up in ICU himself as a patient. His heart was weak and he was being monitored carefully. We had developed a close relationship so I went to see him as soon as I was free that day. His chest was visible beneath the sheet with wires connecting him to the machines. I could see the gray hair covering his chest and looked deeply into his eyes as I did with all my patients. I spoke softly to him. It was an intimate encounter unlike other patient visits.

All of a sudden he pulled me to him and kissed me on the mouth. It startled me and I remember saying to him, "You can't leave now. I just found you again." He smiled at me and nodded. We spent several minutes together looking lovingly at each other. I knew I was very fond of him but had no idea how he felt about me. I've always thought that he kissed me because if he was going to die soon he didn't want to die without having had the chance to kiss a woman. He had begun seminary when he was 14 and had never experienced an intimate relationship with a woman.

Dan was a robust, stubborn Irishman with graying hair cut very short and a square face. He had served in the Navy for 25 years and his posture was very erect. He soon recovered and our ICU encounter was never mentioned. But we fell into an even deeper appreciation and affection for one another. He praised my work and encouraged me continuously. I asked him lots of questions about his ministry and he would follow up with patients to get their reactions to my visits.

As the year of my training progressed, Dan and I spent quite a bit of time together outside of the hospital. I started attending his local parish church and going to the rectory after mass to have coffee and talk on Sunday afternoons. These became regular occurrences for us and an unspoken expectation grew that I would be there. We shared stories about our families, our love of books and movies. He loved to talk about his favorite niece and nephew and their accomplishments. I heard about his other sister's children and came to feel that I was part of their lives.

Once in a while he would take me to dinner or brunch and several times we dined with other people. People began to tell me that he loved me very much. He kissed me occasionally but our love for one another was never mentioned aloud. We fell into an easy pace of forbidden love, having lunch together at the hospital and on Sunday afternoons.

Our relationship continued for many years. I remember one Christmas parked outside the rectory on Christmas Eve looking up at the small decorated tree in the window of his residence. It was adorned beautifully and represented something missing from my life. My tears flowed, aware of what we were both missing by not being able to share our lives together in a broader sense.

This period was incredibly important to my healing. Dan showed me what the purest love was all about. There were no expectations, no sexual innuendos, no pressures in our relationship. We simply loved each other and loved spending time together. Emily Bronte once wrote "Whatever our souls are made of, his and mine are the same." He loved me for just being me, for just *being*. I have said since that he taught me what true love was all about. A chaplain colleague said we were like St. Francis and Clare who spent many years together in chaste partnership.

Once I moved on from the hospital Dan and I stayed in close communication, talking frequently by phone and seeing each other when we could. He was always concerned about my safety and security. He meant the world to me.

****

After several years I again felt called back to Oregon. I missed my kids immensely and decided to return. I found a small cottage to rent and settled into an easy pace. After working part time in an office for a short period I decided to look for a job in hospice. I had loved working with the patients in ICU and thought this would be a good fit for me.

I found a job quickly and began seeing patients on a regular weekly schedule. My days were full and challenging to say the least. I was exhausted at the end of each day but felt more fulfilled than ever before. I knew I was doing what I had been called to do. I deeply cared about my patients and their families and frequently was called on to perform memorial services.

I had witnessed my first death at age 26 when my next door neighbor died while I was visiting. I saw his spirit leave his body and it gave me great peace. While working in hospice I witnessed many deaths and each of them was remarkable in some way. One woman who had been away from the Catholic church for some time died the moment I finished the Lord's Prayer. Another time I told the patient that angels were just waiting to take her home and as I looked around the room, indeed I could see angels hovering near the ceiling. They were hazy images in white robes.

I met lots of wonderful people through hospice, many of whom became lifelong friends. These were mostly the spouses of patients I had cared for. After several years I lost four patients over a Thanksgiving weekend. Three of them I had seen weekly for about a year. Their deaths hit me hard. Soon I decided I needed to be around more people who were going to get well and not die imminently. I knew the director of spiritual care at a local hospital and decided to apply for a position. After an interview with the other chaplains, I was immediately offered the job.

Around this time I decided that I was ready for a lasting relationship. I longed for companionship and although I was still very much in love with Dan, I knew we could never have the kind of relationship I craved. I began to open myself and my heart to finding new love.

Meeting the Love of My Life

In my new job I was assigned to the cardiovascular wing of the hospital, responsible for 72 beds. I visited patients and informed them I was there to support them. Once in a while I received a negative response, but for the most part I saw almost every patient on the two floors. Some I saw daily and others once or twice during their hospitalization. There was a lot of turnover as people were admitted and discharged.

Morning rounds were held every day and we discussed each patient and their situation. One day in late spring the head nurse said, "This one's for you, Margie."

We stood in front of room 28 of the 32 rooms in the horseshoe of cardiac patients. I was surrounded by nurses and social workers, the only chaplain in the group.

"Why?" I asked.

"Because this patient says he came to the hospital to die. He is a dialysis patient and says he is tired and doesn't want to keep going anymore."

"Okay," was all I could think of to say, wondering to myself how I would approach this situation.

After we finished rounds I read the patient's chart and decided to start first with what would probably be my most difficult patient of the day. I entered the room only to find the lead social worker already there.

"You've got to talk to this guy," she said animatedly. "He's great."

"I don't want to interrupt. I can come back," I replied, while walking further into the room. While there I wanted to at least let the patient know who I was and why I was visiting him.

"No, no, please stay," Nancy said. "I think he might really like to talk to you. I can always come back."

So I introduced myself to Tom, a rather large man dressed in a white T-shirt and red silky boxing shorts under the standard ill-fitting hospital gown. He smiled a wide smile and said hello. Very quickly I found myself intrigued as he began quoting the Bible to me.

"You know what I want to ask Jesus when I meet him? I want to know how he divided up all those fish," he said with a grin.

None of my other patients had ever spoken like that, especially on our first meeting. He told me he had been raised a Lutheran but now considered himself a Taoist or Buddhist. He appeared very intelligent and thoughtful.

"Well, I'm very tired. I want to go ahead and die and leave my legacy to my son."

He told me how he had put his son through college and also given him a $20,000 down payment on his first house. It was clear that Tom loved him very much.

As we talked, I declared "Well, I'm not here to change your mind, but I want you to remember that this is a very final decision, not one that you make and then easily change your mind."

We both were aware that once you stop dialysis, especially for someone like Tom whose kidneys had been removed, your body quickly fills with poison and death can be quite painful.

Tom had been diagnosed with polycystic kidney disease years before. It is a hereditary condition. His mother had died from it and a few of his siblings also had the disease. Both of his kidneys had become covered in cysts and were removed in surgery nine years before, weighing 15 and 17 pounds respectively. The average weight of a normal kidney is about 5 or 6 ounces. The only way a person can survive without kidneys is to be on dialysis on a regular schedule.

We chatted for about 15 minutes and I remember saying to him, "Perhaps you have already given your legacy to your son. It sounds like you gave him a wonderful start."

I assured him I would return to see him again. He later told me that his first thought upon meeting me had been, "Oh God, the last thing I need is to talk to a chaplain." Then after I left the room he said to himself, "Those two women were very nice. Why can't I meet a nice woman like that?"

The next day after rounds I found myself in front of Room 28 again wondering what the day would bring. I had since found out from the social worker that Tom was being evicted from his apartment and the hospital care managers were frantically looking for a new place for him to live. I was certain this would contribute to his decision to end his life rather than face a move he didn't have the energy for.

"Hi there," I said as I knocked and entered the room. Tom was again sitting up on his bed, dressed in the same T-shirt and shorts.

"I just heard I'm being evicted. How can they do that while I'm in the hospital? I don't owe them any money. The rent is paid."

"I'm not sure of the circumstances," I said. "That is not part of my job. Have you talked with Nancy again?"

"Yes. But she isn't sure whether she can find anything I can afford. There is a place downtown, an assisted living place that she is checking into."

Meanwhile, I'd been informed by the nurses that if Tom got strong enough to leave the hospital, he would have to go to a nursing home first before being placed.

Our visit was cut short by the aides coming to take him to dialysis. "Will I see you again?"

"Yes, you will. I'll be back later."

Dialysis is a very exhausting process during which the blood is filtered out of the body, cleansed of toxins in a machine and sent back into the veins. Obviously this has to happen over time since the blood cannot all be removed at once. Tom's sessions usually lasted 4-5 hours, after which time he would be weighed and they could determine how much extra fluid had been removed from the body. Because he could not urinate the fluid built up in his body and needed to be eliminated. He endured this process three times a week.

Tom worked for the hospital telecommunications center, helping employees with computer problems. He worked nights and had been doing that for 16 years. He did not exercise and had gotten to the point where he could barely walk from his car to the entrance to the building. He was very overweight. He did dialysis treatments during the day and tried to sleep during sessions to make the time go faster. No wonder the guy was tired!

As each of the next few days passed, I looked forward to seeing him more than most patients. He made me laugh and was very upbeat when we spoke.

Tom was released to a nursing home and I found myself wanting to go see him after work, something that was frowned upon. We were never to follow our patients or keep in touch with them after they left the hospital because it was felt that might cause a codependent relationship and take away our focus from new patients who were entering the hospital each day.

The day after he was discharged from the hospital, I approached one of the nurses and said, "I really liked that guy, you know, the one in 28. I want to go see him."

"Well, go," she said. "Who's going to care? Do you know how many nurses are sleeping with doctors in this place?"

That wasn't anything I wanted to think about, but I did want to see Tom again. I found out where he was staying and decided I would go after work the next day.

I do medical transcription on the side, a part-time job that has lasted for many years. Because I worked full time as a chaplain, I only had time for the transcription work at night or on the weekends. But off to the nursing home I went.

I inquired at the desk which room I needed and lightly knocked on the door. Tom was again sitting on the bed, this time with something new on, another T-shirt and comfy pants. He smiled broadly when I showed up.

"Wow, I didn't expect to see you again!" he exclaimed.

"I just wanted to see how you were doing. Is everything going okay?"

"Yes, I'm feeling a little better. They are trying to get me to do some physical therapy and occupational therapy so they can make sure I can cook for myself." He laughed at that, patting his stomach, "As if that's a problem!"

What I didn't know at that time but would find out later was that Tom was an excellent chef. He had mastered the art on his own and enjoyed teaching these skills to his son. He loved to try out new dishes and had amassed a collection of over 50,000 recipes.

I soon found myself going each evening after work to see Tom then working well into the night with my transcription. That gave me a reason to leave him each evening, but it quickly became apparent that I enjoyed spending time with him.

One evening we were sitting in the lobby of the nursing home on a loveseat. An elderly woman passed us in a wheelchair, making herself go backwards. "Are you two on your honeymoon?" she asked with a high raspy voice, stringing out the syllables.

"No," we both laughed, "we just met." We were sitting together but not touching. This interaction took us by surprise and embarrassed us both. But all we could do was laugh.

We asked around later but no one knew who we were talking about and no one claimed to have seen her before. I decided she had been an angel sent to give us a message.

As I came to know Tom better I found out he had been married three times, the last time 25 years before. He had sworn off women, not wanting to repeat the heartache he had experienced. I had been single for 22 years and married twice. But I was lonely and wanted more companionship in my life.

His roommate at the care facility told him that he was going to marry me.

"No, no, no. I am just looking for a friend," Tom replied jokingly. "Why would you say that?"

"Because if you two saw the way you both light up when you see each other, you would know you were going to marry that girl."

As luck would have it, Tom kissed me a few days later. Nineteen days after our first encounter he asked me to marry him and I said "Yes!" My kids were incredulous, questioning the speed with which this all happened. I laughed and told them we were old and didn't have a lot of time to waste. Obviously I knew that Tom did not expect to live for many more years.

When Tom was released from the nursing home, he moved in with me. After all, he had nowhere to go and we were very much in love. He had few belongings that he needed to bring with him, mostly kitchen items. So one day after being alone for so long, suddenly I had a new man living in my house. I had been afraid that it would be quite a shock to my quiet life, but having him there was wonderful. It was the easiest transition I had ever made.

He went back to work after a few weeks and I was still working full time at the hospital. Our life was full and we laughed a lot. Tom loved to cook and made dinner for me most every night. He didn't want to eat in restaurants, believing that he could come up with a dinner menu better than any chef. We were very affectionate with one another. I was sublimely happy.

Bliss

The next few years were wonderful. We got married in a very small, casual ceremony in the hospital chapel. We broke bread with the guests instead of making a big deal of cake. It was an offering of friendship and union. We were so excited that day. My boss told me I was just like a teenager.

We settled into a quiet life with backrubs and lots of affection. Tom loved to hug and kiss me. He never failed to tell me how much he loved me each day, how beautiful I was and how I was the nicest person he had ever met. I basked in the affection and soaked in the long-needed love. I had never been so happy. I felt very blessed that he had come into my life.

Tom was tall but grossly overweight. He moved slowly or took one of the mobile carts when we went to the store. We teased and laughed a lot and people would stop and stare at us sometimes. He even encouraged me to dance in the aisle of a store to a Christmas carol blaring over the intercom. One guy in Costco said, "Have you two thought of being on TV? You sound just like George Burns and Gracie Allen." They were a comedy team from decades before. We would just smile and keep having fun.

He had a sly grin, big brown eyes and a booming voice. He had had all his teeth pulled many years before because of the risk of infection, something dialysis patients may struggle with. He could speak five languages; had taught making intricate, colorful flies to use to lure the fish while fly fishing and collected hundreds of them for himself. He had made his own glass beads while making jewelry. He even took about 500 pair of earrings to dialysis and gave them to the nurses. He just enjoyed making things. He painted some beautiful scenes that were framed and hung in our house. He did needlepoint and leather work. There were few things he wouldn't tackle. And oh, how he loved to cook.

When we first moved in together I was renting a lovely home that had been owned by a couple, both former hospice patients. I loved the house. It was spacious and in an area of town that I loved. However, Tom thought the yard was too small to have a garden, which he insisted upon. So I began looking at houses, something I also loved to do. Everything I found was not quite right for one reason or another.

One day while driving down the local highway that skirts town, Tom waved his hand and said "why don't you look over that way." The area was close to everything we needed: the post office, grocery store and dialysis center. It just was not a place where I had ever thought about living. Of course I immediately found a house I thought was perfect for us. It had an extra bedroom for an office and a huge yard. It had been owned by a couple who died in their 90s and had lived there for a long time. The yard was also filled with flowers and bushes of every sort.

Tom quickly designed and built four 8 foot by 4 foot raised beds. He made them high enough for him to sit on a board between them and garden on both sides. He loved his garden and tended it every day. He told me that years ago he had always put produce out in front of his house each evening and each morning everything was gone. He was generous that way and wanted to share our abundance. He began planning a huge greenhouse where he could grow and sell plant starts.

He continued to work full time but had asked to begin working days instead of nights so we could be on the same schedule. They made this accommodation begrudgingly since no one else wanted the night shift. They had come to rely on Tom always being there. However, soon Tom was back in the hospital with sepsis. I thought for sure that I would lose him. He spent three days in ICU and I was frantic. He came home on oxygen and we set up the tanks. He was very weak. He then asked if he could work from home remotely. His boss reluctantly agreed but insisted that Tom come in to the office at least one day a week.

After a few months of this Tom was told he was being let go because he was missing too much work. His boss didn't like the fact that he had to leave work early to go to his dialysis treatments. Tom went to him and complained that he was being discriminated against for going to life-saving treatment. His boss agreed with him but said he was going to let him go anyway. When Tom was working nights the fact that he had dialysis during the day didn't disturb any schedules. Once he changed to daytime it became an issue. So after 17 years at the hospital IT center, Tom's career was done.

He decided to fill his extra time making jewelry again. This time instead of making his own beads we began frequenting bead stores and bought many beautiful semi-precious stones. Tom's designs were lovely and he enjoyed doing this immensely. Because he had been awake at night for years he found that was the time he was able to get the most done. I would get up in the morning and find another necklace or two hanging on the curtain rod. He was so proud when I exclaimed how beautiful they all were. He teased me that I would be the best accessorized lady in town.

Dialysis began to be very hard on Tom. His three-times-a-week treatments drained all his energy. His blood pressure was difficult to regulate especially after a session. It would be quite low and the nurses would keep him there until I could arrive. Frequently I was called to come get him instead of him driving home. We lived close to the dialysis center and I got to know all the nurses who worked with him. They were very kind, but obviously concerned. He would come home exhausted but also restless and unable to sleep.

In July, after we had known each other for two years, Tom came home from dialysis on a Friday and went directly to bed. Shortly thereafter he got up and told me he needed to go to the hospital. I asked if he wanted me to call an ambulance or if I could drive him. He was worried that I would get upset like I had been when he was hospitalized before. I assured him I could drive him and off we went. He was placed in a room on the floor where I worked.

Tom was convinced that dialysis was killing him. He told the doctors who were treating him at the hospital that he felt they were taking too much fluid off and he was dehydrated. He did not believe it had anything to do with his heart. It was the weekend and no one seemed too concerned. On Monday he went to the dialysis center in the hospital but they did not remove any fluid. His blood was simply cleansed. When he returned to his room they came in to do an echocardiogram of his heart. He was very uncomfortable and it seemed to take forever.

At the end of the procedure Tom sat up at the end of his bed. I offered to rub his back, a favorite of his. He said yes but wanted to move over to sit on the daybed in the room. He got up with his walker, took two steps and promptly fell head first on the floor. I knew he had died in that moment.

As the nurses and aides all rushed into the room, I went to the hallway and sobbed. His doctor was with me and she asked what I wanted them to do. I knew Tom did not want to be hooked up to tubes and ventilators so I asked them to stop trying to revive him. The doctor told me I was being very brave. She said they could take him to ICU and within three days they would know what was wrong. I declined and told her it wasn't a matter of bravery but of knowing Tom's wishes.

It's now been about six years ago that Tom died. I couldn't figure out why I found it so hard to write this chapter until I realized how much I still miss him. When I obtained Tom's medical records a few weeks after he died, I found that his heart function was only 13 percent. How he had kept going and being cheerful amazed me. He was just that kind of guy.

Everyone told me I had been his angel and given him two more years of life. But I insisted that he had given me a great deal too. I had never felt so loved and he had changed my life through that. I felt confident in my own skin, a feeling that was still relatively new.

Living with Grief and Loss

Over the next few days my daughter helped me move all of Tom's beadwork from the living room into the office. We packed up what we could and it was left for later decisions. I was completely numb. Over the next several weeks, months and even years I avoided all my friends and only talked to my kids. I became a recluse, living day to day in a blur of pain. I couldn't cry but had never felt so sad. It was amazing to me that after only two short years our beautiful relationship had come to an end.

Maybe again it was true that we had learned what we came into each other's lives to learn. Could that be possible? As relationships of every sort, intimate partners, friends and co-workers come into our lives, some of those end in a short period of time. Some may last a lifetime as in marriages that continue for decades.

No one can really know what it is like to experience such deep grief unless they have endured it themselves. That is why so many times we are at a loss for words to say when someone dies. I had lead grief groups through hospice and thought I knew all there was to know about grief. I had studied countless books on the subject. But it quickly became clear that I really didn't know much at all. Tom had been bigger than life and when he was no longer there, the hole was immense. I struggled for months and months to find my way again.

I knew how to take care of the house and the yard and all the paperwork associated with finances. But without his constant love beside me, it was like drudgery to go through the motions. I began to dispose of his clothing and packed things up for his son. I found things in the garage that I didn't even know he owned. I found old mail he had never opened and packed away along with some bills. I closed different accounts he had and tried to sell some of his jewelry. But I never got dressed up or went out except to the grocery store or pharmacy. Insomnia kept me awake most nights for several hours. I was completely unmoored.

****

My life was entirely changed by those two years. After hearing how wonderful and loved I was each day, I had really begun to believe it. Tom's son and daughter-in-law adopted me into their family like I'd been part of it forever. His first granddaughter was born 10 days after Tom died. We all know that he is looking down on her and her new siblings and is so very proud.

I have begun to be more social again, engaging in a course about living life with fun, play and ease. It has enlivened me and introduced me to many wonderful people. I am now in touch with the outgoing person I used to be and my exuberance has returned. My depression has lifted and I feel whole. I am in gratitude each day for every blessing I have in life.

Forgiveness

As I healed it became necessary to look back on my life to reflect if there were still resentments that I held. If it's true that everyone in our lives is there to teach us something, what could I learn from my mother that would be empowering? Embracing forgiveness for my mother as well as myself was a lengthy process. Because I had repressed memories of the molestation, I never had hostile feelings toward my father. I mostly felt sorry for him. He had missed out on having a family, love and commitment. He had died alone in another city, separated from anyone who loved him.

I believe forgiveness began during my early visits with the psychiatrist, but resentment stayed with me for many years. I began to see my mother as a flawed human being. She cared for us as much as she had the capacity to do. She had no sense of self-reflection or how her words and actions hurt others. However, in her own way, she taught me compassion, resilience and openness.

She was determined to make it in a man's world because that was where she found herself. She was left with two children to raise on her own at a time when that was not accepted in society. And she was not very nurturing. If it were not for my grandparents, I'm not sure what would have happened to us.

Forgiveness was revisited each time I guided a women's group since it was a topic covered in the weekly design, but that focused on the group participants. It was harder to focus on forgiveness of myself. I had to accept the fact that many times in my life I had been a brat. I strongly resented Mother's influence over my life with our opposing views on politics, racial equality, sexual orientation, etc. I spent many years questioning my own beliefs because they were so contrary to hers. Although my brother and I were taught to be independent, we were not encouraged or told that we could accomplish anything we set our minds to. I often wondered how I would have turned out if Mother had actually been able to nurture and encourage me.

I was terrified of my Mother until I was about age 50. That was when I came to full acceptance of my height, my weight and my abundance of love for others. In Robin Sharma's book *The 5 AM Club*, Mr. Riley says: "Comparison is the thief of joy...Someone will always have more fortune, fame and stuff than you do."

Mother never accepted any of my career choices until I became a chaplain. Then she began to brag about me to her friends, feeling that I had a profession that was worthy of praise or one that would be recognized by her friends as such. She never gave up the need to have others look upon her with approval.

Studying as a chaplain with its rigorous training included intense self-reflection. It found me crying frequently. I think it was then that I truly let go of all my hatred and rage. After the stroke I looked around one day and realized I no longer felt depressed. Turning my life over to God's direction certainly helped everything. I had forgiven both my husbands for their earlier transgressions and my mother for not loving me the way I wanted or needed. I realized they all had loved me in their own ways.

One of the things I remember while working in hospice was a specific graveside service I was asked to perform. The daughter had had a very conflicted relationship with her mother and told me her mother had been very cruel. I asked the angels to help me write something that would be meaningful for the daughter and perhaps reframe the situation. I was left with something that touched me.

I told the gatherers: When she was cruel, she taught you compassion. When she was stubborn, she taught you patience. When she discouraged you, she taught you self-reliance. I don't remember the exact words now, but it helped me reframe my relationship with my mother too. The daughter was very grateful and told me she would like to participate in any forgiveness workshop I offered.

Each time I did another personal growth program, forgiveness of myself and others always managed to arise. I realized how much I had hurt other people throughout my life. I suffered from dissociation and sometimes said things that were out of context or misunderstood. I pushed away friends when I began to feel they needed me too much. It took many layers of self-forgiveness to get to the core of my pain.

In his book *The 5 AM Club*, Sharma relates a story about a character he calls the Spellbinder. In a speech to a large audience, the Spellbinder says:

> "And yes, I am aware that there are also many in this room who are currently leading lives you love. You're an epic success in the world, fully on your game and enriching your families and communities with an electricity that borders on otherworldly. Nice work. Bravo. And, yet, you too have experienced seasons where you've been lost in the frigid and dangerous valley of darkness. You, too, have known the collapse of your creative magnificence as well as your productive eminence into a tiny circle of comfortableness, fearfulness and numbness that betrayed the mansions of mastery and reservoirs of bravery inside of you. You, too, have been disappointed by the barren winters of a life weakly lived. You, too, have been denied many of your most inspired childhood dreams. You, too, have been hurt by people you trusted. You, too, have had your ideals destroyed. You, too, have had your innocent heart devastated, leaving your life decimated, like a ruined country after ambitious foreign invaders infiltrated it."[xxxi]

For years I had lived in the valley of darkness that had surrounded me and held me fixed in my pain and resentment. Forgiveness was the single thing that brought me out of that.

Several years ago my first husband's second wife died, he called me and said "I need a friend and you were the only person I could think of." I was trained as a chaplain so I just listened. This was how I approached our first several conversations. We talked on the phone over the next number of years and began to heal our differences. He told me he believed all my unhappiness in our marriage was because of him. I explained that I had been suicidal since grandma's death and he began to understand all the hurt feelings I had endured.

Twenty-four years after our breakup husband number two contacted me. He cried and apologized for hurting me. It was a sincere move toward forgiveness. He still calls periodically.

Forgiveness is not about condoning or approving of anyone's behavior. We are the ones who are helped by forgiving others, by letting go of hurt in order to heal ourselves. The hurt and anger can fester inside of us and cause great stress, which in turn takes a toll on our bodies. Lack of forgiveness can manifest in addictive behavior, drinking or doing drugs to lessen the pain. It is not until we can forgive ourselves and others that we are truly free. Some people have said forgiveness is an inside job. It is for ourselves, not anyone else. It truly frees us, lightens our load and gives us peace. Others are not affected by our hurt feelings. We are. Forgiveness is all about loving ourselves.

Gratitude

I am very grateful that I did not commit suicide. I am left with a deep sense of gratitude. The depression and pain was overwhelming, but somehow I kept going. I found trained people to talk to. I took medication. I slowly began to make friends, people who care about me without me doing anything. That was amazing coming from a place of feeling like I needed to pay for lunch in order to get someone to spend time with me.

I didn't embrace my true calling in life until after age 50. I didn't meet the love of my life until I was 63. These things would not have happened had I ended my life many years ago.

One thing I know for certain is that the only reason I am still living is because of God. God, or whatever name you place on the Eternal Being, remained patient. There were years that I stayed away from church, drank too much and had affairs. But God was always there, just waiting for me to come back. The fact that I can say my kids are what kept me alive is true. But they came from God. They are amazing human beings who love me too. And luckily they did not have to bear the burden of having a mother who killed herself, forever wondering why.

So if you are thinking of suicide, please take a moment and find someone to talk to. There are people who will listen to your pain and not judge you. If you think you might need medication to control your depression, then by all means go see a doctor. I spent years in therapy throughout my life and I still take antidepressants to this day. This is nothing to be ashamed of, although there are some who would like you to believe that.

I have long believed that we are all one. We are all the same regardless of our skin tone, wrinkles or beauty. We are the same no matter how tall or short we are or how much we weigh. We each have dreams and desires, challenges and pain. Look around you. God is everywhere, in everything. We need to look for the deep connection between us rather than seeking division. We can change our lives just by changing our minds.

I recently watched a YouTube video of Neal Donald Walsch, who wrote the famous *Conversation with God* series. He was speaking on "Our Role In Evolution." In that interview I heard him say that our basic instinct is not survival, but rather divinity. I was struck by that statement. He likened it to walking by a burning building and hearing a baby cry. If survival were our basic instinct we would run in the other direction, but most people would, without hesitation, run into the burning building to save the baby.

You have that potential just as much as anyone else. What if your one purpose in life was to save another person? If you are gone, who will take on that task? Anyone?

Each one of us is a unique individual, created by God. Although you might not believe it, that divine spark is still within you. You can find it again. You have much to offer. Whether you believe it or not, you are resilient and strong. You have had dreams of what life could look like. It still can if you stick around long enough to find it. You can withstand more than you think. Please stay. The world needs you.

Resources: National Suicide Prevention Lifeline: 800-273-8255
TTY Crisis Line: 800-799-4889
Trevor Project for LGBT Teen Community: 866-488-7386